M000113830

My
Life's
JOURNEY

Shirley Hammermeister

ISBN 978-1-0980-8266-6 (paperback)
ISBN 978-1-0980-8267-3 (digital)

Copyright © 2020 by Shirley Hammermeister

All rights reserved. No part of this publication may be reproduced, distributed, or transmitted in any form or by any means, including photocopying, recording, or other electronic or mechanical methods without the prior written permission of the publisher. For permission requests, solicit the publisher via the address below.

Christian Faith Publishing, Inc.
832 Park Avenue
Meadville, PA 16335
www.christianfaithpublishing.com

Printed in the United States of America

To my children, Mark, Marsha, and Kathy;
to my grandchildren, Anna, Chris, James,
Leah, Jordan, Eric, and Andrew;
and my great-grandchildren, Jonathan and Emma Jane.

INTRODUCTION

I will soon be eighty-three years of age and I thank God every day for each and every year he has given me. The purpose of my book is to let my family—my children, grandchildren, and great-grandchildren—know what my life was like growing up, the mistakes I made and what I have overcome through prayer and God's grace. Also how much our world has changed in a short period of time.

Years ago, life was so much simpler. No one was in a hurry. People took time to enjoy the beauty of nature. You always had time to help a neighbor and visit friends and relatives.

This book is also to let everyone know that regardless of what happens in your life, with Jesus Christ as your Lord and Savior, there is nothing you can't be forgiven for. Ask for his help and he is there. I have experienced it more than once in my lifetime. There is nothing you can't do if you ask for his guidance and help. Even write a book at an advanced age!

Chapter

1

As I worked on my book, I realized just how fragile life is. The years have flown by. Now in my eighties looking back through the years, I see so many things were God's working hands. He was there keeping me from harm's way. I have also been guided through books, dreams, people, sermons, and letters. What an awesome God we serve.

My life began at Deaconess Hospital, Detroit, Michigan, in September 1937. Those were not easy years for my parents, Albert and Esther.

My mom and dad were both raised on dairy farms in Engadine, Michigan. At age sixteen, my dad drove horses for a lumber camp. Shortly after, he struck out for Chicago working in the steel mills and lived with a cousin. My mother had a very traumatic beginning when her mother suffered a nervous breakdown and spent the next thirty-six years of her life in a mental hospital. My mother was four years old when her mother was forced to leave her family.

Life at home was hard as the oldest sibling was only twelve years old at the time. My Aunt Eleanor took over the household duties and left home by age sixteen. At age thirteen, my mother went to Detroit. Looking much older and lying about her age, she found employment with a Jewish family as nanny/housekeeper. She earned three dollars a week. There she learned to cook, clean, and do all household chores.

My dad moved to Detroit and lived with his only sister, Elsie. He worked at Hudson Motor Car Co. My parents dated and on August 3, 1935, my mother, age sixteen, and my dad, age twenty-six, were married. My mother had a lace dress. She told me it cost her a week's wages to pay for her hat. In those days, the bride had a huge bouquet of flowers to carry. Hers was no exception.

Those were the post-Depression years, and money was tight. My parents rented apartments for a few years and later rented a house. Mom was a stay-at-home housewife.

I was the oldest grandchild on my dad's side of the family. My Aunt Elsie had a son, Ronald, a year after I was born. My family would spend a lot of time at their house and they at ours. We played a lot in the sandbox, letting our imagination build all sorts of things. We would play games but loved to roller-skate most of all. I wore dresses most of the time, so needless to say I had a lot of scabby knees from falling while roller-skating.

Then came December 7, 1941. My memories of Detroit didn't really start until World War II. I was four years old at the time. I had a new baby brother born March 1941. Many things changed. Hudson's quit making cars, and the factory made the tail of the B-29. Ninety-nine percent of the workers were women, whom my dad supervised.

Food was rationed and families were issued coupon books to purchase items such as sugar, etc. Candy bars were rationed as they were sent to the men overseas. I remember going to the butcher shop with my mother and seeing a long string in the air, stretching the length of the room. On it were hanging whole chickens. Other meats were in a showcase.

Women didn't wear nylons in those days because the nylon was used to make parachutes for the military. Cosmetic companies came up with a lotion tinted to look like nylon. It was okay to wear in the winter, but during the summer, it sure did smudge.

Many foods were scarce, but come holiday time like Easter, Thanksgiving, and Christmas, the aunts, uncles, and cousins got together for a big meal and visiting. Most of the relatives lived in Detroit, so travel was not a problem.

One of the first things I remember Mom buying for me was a high metal chair. I was only three at the time but remember the hardware store with its two large windows in front and a door between them. The floor was made of wood. The metal chair was painted green. Many years later, and many coats of paint later, it served all four of my siblings and was used for all the grandchildren. It found a final home in my daughter Marsha's kitchen, where it remains today.

In spite of the war years, I will always remember the wonderful Christmases I had. My most memorable Christmas was walking toward our Christmas tree. There was a maple table with two armchairs, a blue-and-white tablecloth, and a set of porcelain dishes with a blue-and-white design. Sitting in one of the chairs was a beautiful slim doll with brown hair. She was wearing a red velvet outfit trimmed in white fur. She also had a white fur muff on one hand. I named her Donna Lou. My aunt Erna had bought me a metal stove with enamel pots and pans on it. Next to the stove was another doll with blond hair that became Donna Lou's buddy. She had a porcelain face too. I named her Betty Lou. The table lasted through all my siblings and my children, nieces, and nephews. It is now at home with granddaughter Jordan.

During the war years, we had curfews at night. As soon as it was dark, all lights went out, and families lit a candle here and there. It kept the enemy from knowing where the cities were in case of bombing. My brother was four months old when my dad put my mother, brother, and I on a train headed for the Upper Peninsula of Michigan. That was where my grandparents lived in Engadine. It was July 1941, and the train was loaded with servicemen going home on furlough before going overseas. My mother had one big suitcase for us; she had to sit on the suitcase in the aisle because there were no seats available. A woman held her son on her lap so I could sit beside her. I was almost four years old at the time but can still see so vividly all the soldiers sitting and standing.

That summer, my mother helped my grandmother with the garden produce, both canning and cooking. One day while Mom was hanging clothes on the line, a big white rooster started chasing me. I ran screaming toward my mother. My grandmother grabbed the rooster by the legs and took him to the chopping block. We had chicken noodle soup that day for lunch. I can remember looking into the bowl with a big smile on my face and said, "You will never chase me again."

It was a memorable time in my life because I could watch my grandpa feed the pigs, chop wood, and do various things on the farm. It was so different from life in Detroit. By Labor Day, we were back in Detroit.

I started kindergarten at St. Thomas Lutheran School, which was within walking distance from home. In those days, it was safe to let children walk to school. We would have Bible study before resuming our other classes. I treasure those years because I never forgot the stories. It was the beginning of my walk with God.

As long as I can remember, my one dream was to become a registered nurse. A lady living in the apartment above us was an RN and sometimes she would let me wear her starched white cap.

The last street we lived on in Detroit was Holcomb. I remember the upright, black telephones with a mouthpiece you could talk into. You could dial your number from a round piece at the base of the phone. You held another piece to your ear to hear the voice on the other end. I still remember the phone number. It was Ivanhoe 8709. How the phones have changed through the years.

We lived in a White neighborhood but had one African American family directly across the street from us. Their youngest daughter was a little older than me, but she would invite me over to her house for a tea party. The family was very nice, and my dad often referred to him as "the only White man on the block."

One of my most memorable memories was the end of World War II. There were people celebrating everywhere. A family friend, Ed Golder, picked us up in his car that night. By that time, I had another new brother, Allan, three months old. Ed had a metal washtub attached to the back bumper of the car and he was driving down the streetcar tracks. I was looking out the back window of the car watching the sparks fly all over from the tub on the tracks. By the time we got home, the bottom of the washtub was burned out. We lived less than a block from Gratiot Avenue. The day after the war was over, I walked to the corner and all I could see were men dressed in white coveralls pushing brooms and picking up the garbage from the big celebration the night before. Lots of trucks were loaded with all the debris.

10

During the war years, my mother would often go to the movie theater where you could purchase a set of satellite dishes, a few pieces at a time, at little cost. She ended up with service for eight. Seventy-five years later, they are in the possession of my youngest brother.

Both of my parents, having been raised in the Upper Peninsula of Michigan, wanted to get out of the city and move back to farm country. During the war years, they purchased a forty-acre farm next to my grandparents. One month after the war ended, we moved to Engadine about three weeks before my ninth birthday; it was there that I spent the remainder of my growing years.

My grandparents gave my mom and dad four cows and some chickens to get started. On our farm we had a small barn with stalls for cows and attached to it was a section with a hay mow. On the other side was a building for young stock and another attached building that was a chicken coop. The barn stood on a little hill that slanted down to a spring-fed creek. On the opposite side of the creek, on another little hill, stood our ol' green house. We had a small back-yard and another building that was our woodshed with a narrow, attached garage.

My parents milked the cows by hand. We had no electricity in the barn, so we used kerosene lanterns. We had no running water in the house but there was a pump not far from the back door outside. During the winter, the creek was frozen over, so the cows couldn't get water to drink. My brother Don and I would take turns pumping water into a big watering tank. It seemed like each cow drank forever. Our hands would get so cold pumping the water. We also had an outdoor toilet well-equipped with catalogs.

Now that the war was over, the car factories were reconverting the plants to making automobiles again. To help out financially, my dad went back to Detroit, lived with his sister, and continued working at Hudson's. The months ahead were hard on my mother. She had to milk and feed the cows, chickens, and pigs. She had three children to care for besides cooking and baking. That is when she taught me how to cook and bake.

On Halloween night, the neighbor kids tied an old telephone pole across the driveway. Mom had to cut the wire and drag the pole out of the way so she could get out of the driveway. That topped the frustration. That evening, she drove three miles into town where the only telephone was located at the grocery store. She called my dad and asked him to come home. Somehow they would manage without the extra money from the shop. He quit the factory job, came home, and once again our family was all together.

Being the oldest child, a girl, I grew up in a hurry. By age nine, I was helping take care of my brother Allan, who was still on the bottle and in diapers. I helped plant and harvest the garden. Everything had to be canned at that time because it was before freezers came into being. I used the ol' ringer washing machine. We had a metal stand that held two washtubs full of water for rinsing and hung the clothes out to dry. In the winter, the clothesline was strung back and forth in the dining room where the clothes were hung to dry.

By my taking over those chores, it freed my mom up to help my dad work in the fields, clear land, and work behind the hay loader spreading hay on the wagon. My brother Don was very young, age six or seven, and would drive the horse pulling the hay into the mow with a huge fork attached to a rope. Mom would set the fork into the hay on the wagon, the horse pulled the rope going into the mow, and my dad spread the hay in the mow. It was hard work and took lots of time.

We had a machine called a binder. It would cut, bundle, and tie the oats stalks and drop them to the ground. Then you gathered the bundles with a pitchfork and stood them up like a teepee (which we called doodles). There might be six to eight sheaves in a doodle.

To harvest the oats, ten to twelve area farmers would go from farm to farm as a big work crew. My brother Don and I drove the tractor while the men would pitch the sheaves onto the wagon. The wagon would be pulled in front of the thrashing machine. One guy would pitch the sheaves into the thrasher, which separated the oats from the straw. The straw was blown into a pile and the oats went into gunnysacks, which men carried on their shoulders, dumping it into the granary bin. I would help shovel the oats to the side of the bin so it could be filled. We never thought about wearing a mask to keep from inhaling all the dust. By the end of the day, we were covered in dust and very itchy.

The year I was twelve, my brother and I stayed home from school to drive tractor for the threshing crew, which consisted of about fifteen men. It was my twelfth birthday. We were at the Nichols farm. Ida was a small woman, less than five feet tall, but could she work. She put out the big meal for the men, and we worked until milking time. Later that evening, she came over to our house with a decorated angel food cake for my birthday. I never forgot what she did for me besides all the work she had at home, including milking the cows.

Soon after my dad left Detroit and came back to the farm, he installed a hand water pump at the kitchen sink, which saved a lot of back-and-forth walking to carry water from outside. We had a big Kalamazoo woodstove in the kitchen for cooking. It had four plates for cooking and a water reservoir on the right side. There would always be hot water for washing. On laundry days, we had a big copper tub we put on the stove to heat the water for the washing machine. The oven was big. We had a big kitchen, so there was a lot of room to work in when it was canning time. The ol' green house was special to the boys and me I think because of all the good memories we had living there. As adults, one or all of us would dream about the ol' green house from time to time.

The average farm was about eighty acres to one hundred sixty acres. By the time I was age twelve, most farmers owned at least one tractor. Every farm had a car or a vehicle of some sort. Our neighbors, the Legault family, had a jeep-type vehicle which we called "the Doodlebug." On Sunday morning, Bud, the oldest son, would help Mom into the open-top Doodlebug. She would use one hand to hold her hat on and the other to hold on to the seat, and down the road they would go; the three miles into town where the Catholic Church was located. When we first moved to Engadine, we had a Hudson car, but by the time I was twelve we had a brand-new Studebaker.

When we first moved to Engadine in 1945, there were only three churches in the area. The Catholic and Methodist churches were in town, and Bethlehem Lutheran Church was three miles into the country. It was different from the Lutheran Church we attended in Detroit. The men sat in pews on the right side of the aisle, and the women and kids sat on the left. There were two services, with the early service being held in German and the second service in English. My being the oldest grandchild, my grandmother learned how to speak English. I have always regretted the fact that I didn't have her talk to me in German so I could learn the language. I do remember a few words but not enough to carry a conversation.

Between ages nine through twelve, I would pedal my bike on gravel road three miles to church in the summer to Bible study. The classes were Monday through Friday from 9:00 a.m. till 12:00 noon. I was confirmed on April 2, 1950.

During those first years on the farm, my parents sold cream, which would be put in a five-gallon can and kept cold in a tank of water. It was shipped by train to Sault Ste. Marie, Michigan, to the creamery about a hundred miles away. My brother Don and I looked forward to driving into town to deliver the tagged cans of cream to the depot for delivery to the Soo. Don and I could go inside the depot, where Mr. Hollsted had a Beeman's gum machine. It held individual packets of gum with two pieces per packet. The wrappers were in five different colors, so each week we would pick a different color. Each packet cost us a cent. We would make those two small squares of gum last us from one week to the next.

We had a town hall in Engadine that was used for putting on our Christmas programs at school since the school did not have a gymnasium. The hall was used for different occasions through the year. During the summer, a man, Mr. Beech, showed movies on Saturday night. We would sit on backless wooden benches and enjoy watching the old *Tarzan* movies or Westerns with Tom Mix or the Lone Ranger.

The summer I was eleven, my Uncle Otto, who was a carpenter, and Aunt Eleanor came up from Detroit for the summer, and he built cabinets in our big kitchen. We had a modern sink and running water! We didn't need the pantry anymore, and that fall my dad put in a bathroom. Wow! Were we getting modern. No more outdoor toilet.

About that time, we had electricity in the barn and my parents purchased a Surge milking machine. No more milking by hand. Our dairy herd increased. We no longer shipped cream to the Soo but sent our milk to the local cheese factory located across the road from our church.

During those years, farmers did not work on Sunday. We attended church, and after services, we would decide whose house to visit. We had no phones. Everyone would go home from church, have dinner, and then the whole family would get in the car and visit somewhere. In the summer, the girls would play jacks on the sidewalk (if we had sidewalk), playhouse with our dolls, have tea parties, etc. The boys usually played softball or baseball. In the winter, we would ice skate or go tobogganing.

All the farmers had small farms, so the neighbors lived close by. Most families had from five to twelve children. The Legault family lived directly across the road from us. The Vallier family had twelve children and lived about a quarter of a mile from us. Once the snow fell, there was always something to do. We had a creek that flowed between our house and barn, so we had to cross the bridge to get from one to the other. The creek flowed across the road to a big field on the Legault property. Every fall, a big pond would form in the Legault field to the road. We would bank the snow up around the pond, which gave us a nice big area to ice skate.

Our three families would get together after evening chores. We would carry lanterns to four different places on the ice for light. We would skate until our legs couldn't hold us up anymore and then we would sit around a bonfire built by one of the parents. We roasted marshmallows and sometime hot dogs. On weekends, we would work on building snow forts. Sometimes the walls were quite high. We had some pretty good snowball fights around the forts.

The Vallier farm had a big hill in their field across the road from their farm. That is where we would play "king of the hill." That too could get rough at times, especially if we sank into the snow. Sometimes the snow was wetter than other times. We would also toboggan down the hill, just missing the line fence.

After we tired ourselves out, we would head over to the Valliers' big house across the road from the big hill. Mrs. Vallier had the patience of a saint. About ten of us would come into the back porch and shed our wet jackets, snow pants, and boots, which meant there was always water to mop up. About then the hot chocolate, popcorn, or fudge was prepared. We would play Monopoly, Fish, Old Maid, and Chinese checkers. That is how our weekends and many evenings were spent. We tried to do our homework at school so we could have the evening free for play. The Legault kids and my brother Don and I would grab our lanterns and toboggans and head for home after a fun-filled night. The forts would stand until the snow melted in the spring, and we skated until the ice wasn't safe anymore. We had some nasty falls but all during those years, no one ever broke a bone.

When we didn't have crops to put in, there was usually one day a week I could ride my bike to my cousin Eunice Matchinske's, who lived three miles away on McKelvey Road; or the home of Janet Yeske, who lived on what is now M117. I could take the shortcut on Alley Road, which bordered our eighty acres of land.

About that time, brother number three arrived. Gary was born on Good Friday. Mothers who had just given birth stayed in the hospital about five days back then. That Easter Sunday, Popsie's Aunt Martha and Uncle Dan were visiting from Detroit. After church, Popsie invited them to dinner at our house. My Uncle Ervin, who was living with us for a while, had given my mother an electric roaster for Christmas. Mom would always fix dinner in the roaster before going to church, so when we came home it didn't take long to sit down to dinner. Mom was a Sunday school teacher. That meant getting chores done very early on Sunday so we could attend Sunday school before church.

By that time, families sat together in the pews, for which we were all glad. Mom taught Sunday school for twenty-three years. That particular Sunday, I had fixed a pork roast, mashed potatoes, gravy, and green beans, and a cream pie for dessert. Aunt Martha was amazed that at age twelve I could put out a meal like that. Later that afternoon, we went to Newberry, where my dad visited Mom as no kids were allowed in the hospital.

One summer, we didn't get much rain. I remember the oats crop was about ready to harvest. During the night, we could hear a noise outside but didn't really know what it was. The next morning when we got up, we were heartsick at what we saw. The oats field by the barn was completely stripped of oats; just the stems were standing. Grasshoppers had gone through during the night and stripped the oats off the stem. It was the only time I ever saw my dad cry. Our total oats crop was gone.

We had no TVs, so we just had the radio to listen to. My mother would embroider or crochet doilies and sell them, and I also learned to embroider and crochet.

One thing I will never forget is the German weddings when I was about twelve. There were no town halls at the time, so after the wedding in church, you went to the bride's or groom's house. Their families moved the furniture out of the house, brought in church banquet tables and chairs, and you ate in one or two (sometimes three) rooms depending on the size of the room. After the meal, you went to a building outside where they held the dance. Usually the music was an accordion or a fiddle.

Earl Fergin and my mother were two accordion players. They usually took turns playing. The music went on until it was time to go home and milk the cows. Very seldom did a wedding only last one day; most were two-day weddings. My great uncle's daughter got married in a two-day affair, and the next day was the parents' wedding anniversary, so the celebration went into the third day. My mother and Earl played their accordion until about 4:30 a.m. and then went home to milk the cows and get a couple hours' sleep. Usually by noon, everyone was coming back for the second-day party. One particular farmer never went home for two days but slept in the apple orchard.

Mom and Popsie bought another eighty acres down the road from some people called Richards—thus it was referred to as the Richard Eighty. All of our land was very stony, and we used a dray-like stone boat to put the rocks on as we drove over the fields picking them up. We would find a spot for our stone pile, which sometimes got very big. We might have as many as three to four stone piles in one field, depending on the size of the field.

The Legault farm across the road was sold to Betty and Lawrence Vallier. That is where they started their family of three boys and a girl. I was old enough to babysit; it was convenient for me to babysit for them since I just had to walk across the road. I also had the experience of taking care of babies, so I made a little spending money that way.

One day in early spring, we still had to have a fire in the stove to take the chill out of the house. Lawrence got the fire going in the kitchen stove, and the next thing he knew they had a fire inside the wall. There was no wind that day and it was a slow-burning fire. We had no telephones, so Betty got in the car, pulled into each farmer's yard blowing the horn, and yelled that the house was on fire. My parents were the first people to get there. My mother carried a full mattress out of the house, on her back, by herself. Later, I remember her saying she had no idea how she did it. It didn't take long for the other farmers to drop everything and rush to their farm. Every piece of furniture was saved from that fire. (We had no fire department at that time either.)

When I was fifteen, my parents bought a riding horse from a cousin who lived in Manistique. They paid a hundred fifty dollars for him. His name was Smokey. We would ride him to take the cows to and from where they would pasture during the day at the Richard Eighty. He wasn't ridden as much as he should have been and was very spunky. After about a year, my dad sold him because I couldn't handle him anymore.

In June 1953, our family expanded once again with the addition of my sister, Peggy. There were now five siblings. Mom had a hard time getting Peggy on a formula that agreed with her. About that time, I was not feeling well; I had chills but no flu symptoms. Mom took Peggy to the doctor and had me hold her on the way to the clinic.

After the doctor checked Peggy out, Mom told the doctor how I had been feeling. He checked me over and also had me do blood work. As soon as he saw the results, he told mom I needed emergency appendectomy surgery. Mom drove home with Peggy, and I was admitted to the hospital. About two hours later, I had surgery. The appendix was ready to burst, and I had never even had an attack! That was the first of many divine interventions in my life, but at the time I didn't know it.

Chapter 2

I never had a date during my first one and a half years of high school. I often wondered what was wrong with me that boys didn't ask me out. It took fifty plus years for me to find out my mother was the cause. Several guys told me, after all those years, that they were afraid of my mother.

One night during my sophomore year, Richard and Robert Hammermeister (twins and relatives on my mother's side of the family) came over in the early evening while we were cutting and wrapping beef for the freezer. They asked if I could go to the show with them and Elaine Stelter, whom we knew very well. Both boys were home on furlough from the Army. Robert had met Elaine earlier when he was at the Coast Guard Station in the Soo. They were both visiting their Aunt Ida, who was like a second mother to the boys.

Richard and I hit it off right from the start. We were a foursome for the next four nights until Richard had to report back to Granite City, Illinois. When he left, he told me he hoped to marry me someday. We wrote to each other, but it didn't last long because my mother said if I didn't break it off, they would not pay for my schooling. I had hoped to be a registered nurse someday. Back in those days, you did what your parents commanded you to do and you did it. I sent Richard a "Dear John" letter but also stated in the letter I would always love him.

The summer between my junior and senior year of high school, I worked at the Hiawatha Cub dining hall. Two other classmates of mine worked there too. It was my first job away from home. The club was only about six miles from home, but we were given cabins to stay in, which made it easier for us since we had to be on the job about the time our parents would be in the barn milking cows.

Toward the end of my senior year, I put my application in to Deaconess Hospital (where I was born) in Detroit and applied for nurse training. I had all the required shots, and the end of April I went to Detroit for all of my testing. At that time it was a three-year program to be a registered nurse. I graduated from high school, and my mother was one of the chaperons on our senior trip to Milwaukee. When we came home, I had a letter waiting from the hospital saying they couldn't accept me because my math grade wasn't high enough.

That summer, my Aunt Erna was visiting with my family from Stillwater, Oklahoma. She invited me to go back to Oklahoma with her, work in their bakery, and attend college at Oklahoma A&M. I decided to move to Tulsa with my parents' blessing. We would be driving back to Oklahoma. While crossing on the ferry (the Straits of Mackinac), my throat started getting sore. By the time we got to Detroit where we stayed with another aunt, I felt sick and could hardly swallow. The next morning, I was too sick to get out of bed. I ran a high fever, and my gums were swollen over my teeth.

The next day, my Aunt Eleanor took me to the doctor. I was diagnosed with trench mouth. The doctor thought I might have gotten it from a dirty glass I had drunk out of the night before when I had gone to a dance at Hancock's. Aunt Erna had to go back to Tulsa without me. That was my first encounter of how God works in one's life. It was a trip I was not to take. Deep down in my spirit, I knew it was God who intervened. I didn't understand why but knew there had to be a good reason I was not to make that move.

That summer, I worked as a waitress at Beaudions Café in Naubinway, from July to mid-October. I loved the work and to this day am grateful for the job and the friendship with Bob Beaudion, who was my boss. We still reminisce about those years.

Early October, I took a Greyhound bus to Lansing, Michigan, where I lived with an aunt and uncle. In those days, coming from the UP there were no jobs so you either got married or went downstate to find work. Of my fifteen classmates, at least ten of us chose to find work in Lansing. Most of the boys worked in factories. One girl worked for the phone company, another insurance. I ended up with a job for the state. I started working at Secretary of State, which was within walking distance from where I lived. There was no chance of advancement, and I didn't care for my boss, who "didn't like people from the UP." I applied for a transfer to the Michigan State Police Headquarters in East Lansing.

I was on the waiting list for seven months when my transfer went through. My boss didn't fight the transfer. I had grown up knowing how to respect people, so I was really sticking my neck out at age eighteen, but I did have the pleasure of telling her, "It will take a while, but someday you will realize you lost the best hardworking employee you ever had." In most places, they hired you when you said you were from the UP because almost anyone who came from the UP was brought up to be a hard worker.

While I was at Sec of State, a group of us girls walked to a restaurant for lunch one day. One of the girls with us was Black. She was a sweet lady and a few years older than me. When we started walking, the White girls were walking double and here was Lila walking by herself. Having been raised in an area where we didn't have or even see Blacks, I couldn't understand why no one was walking with her. I walked with her, and we had a good conversation.

About six months later, one of my friends from work, Marion, wanted to drive to Nashville and take in the *Grand Ole Opry*. I was game to go since I loved country music and wanted to travel. Marion and I were walking down the street in Nashville. Two Black men were walking toward us. As we got closer to them, they stepped off the sidewalk onto the grass to let us pass. I can remember turning and looking back. I saw them step back onto the sidewalk. My heart ached that they felt they had to do that. I was shocked to think that in 1958, things like that were still taking place. Little did I know that, as time went on, the very best friend I would ever have would be Black.

Being in the city was a whole new life for me. I enjoyed going downtown and just window-shopping. In those days, the ladies still wore hats to church so there were a lot of hat stores. I loved going into them and looking at all the different styles. I also enjoyed the old-fashioned soda fountains. Usually after I finished looking around, I would have a chocolate soda at one of the five-and-dimes still in existence. To this day, I love my chocolate and chocolate sodas.

There were five of us who went home for Christmas that first year after graduation. We had to wait until the last of the five were out of work before we could head for home because none of us had been at our jobs long enough for vacation time. The last ferry at the Straits of Mackinac left at midnight, and the next ferry wouldn't run until 6:00 the next morning. The five of us were in one car and we put "the pedal to the metal," arriving at the dock just as the last ferry pulled out. It was Christmastime, cold with lots of snow on the ground, and there we sat until 6:00 a.m. Construction had started on the Mackinac Bridge earlier that year. When I finally got home, I vowed I would never complain about the fare to cross on the bridge when it was completed regardless of how much it cost. To this day, I have never complained.

The bridge was completed in November 1957. I worked at State Police Headquarters through June of 1959. Of all the jobs I have had in my lifetime, I still say working at the Police Post was the best job I ever had. By then, I had dated a few times but nothing serious.

About that time, I was having a lot of issues with my sinuses. After much doctoring, my doctor told me to go back to the UP, where I could be healthy again. I used a lot of sick days because of the sinus problems.

My brother Don graduated from high school in May, and I went home for his graduation. At the graduation dance held at Hancock's on Millecoquin Lake, I met Larry Anderson. We danced a lot that night, and he took me home after the dance. I went back to Lansing to finish up my last three weeks of work with the State Police. After I came back home, Larry and I continued to see each other. Larry played baseball, so I attended a lot of games.

In August, I flew to Tulsa, Oklahoma, to spend two weeks with Aunt Erna. She and her husband owned a bakery there. It was the wettest summer in history. While there, we encountered a problem with snakes. On Monday morning, upon leaving the house, we left the main door open with just the screen door. She lived in a country setting with a big river flowing nearby. While we were gone, a thunderstorm went through with strong winds. Upon arriving home, I walked into the dining area where my fold-up bed was standing in a corner. On the floor behind it was a coiled white-mouth water moccasin.

Aunt Erna had lived in Tulsa for years and until then hadn't even seen a snake. She went to the shed and came back armed with a spade and a hoe. She slid the bed out and, with the shovel, came down on the snake's back breaking its spine. She had me hack away at its head with the hoe, and before long the head was barely attached.

The following Friday, we turned on the AC and went out the door near her bedroom. Upon reentering the room, there stretched out across her two bedroom windows was another snake! This one was green in color with white spots. She proceeded to get our "weapons" again but this time swinging the shovel against the windowsill. It did nothing to the snake but hold it down while it stretched itself around the shovel handle. Using the hoe, I hacked the tar out of the sill and the snake's head. We called the police. They came out to see the snake and told us it was a chicken snake and not poisonous. To this day, I keep my distance from snakes.

That Sunday I was to fly out of Tulsa back to Michigan. The airport had so much water on it that my flight was the last one out that day. I came back to Engadine and helped Mom can and freeze fresh fruit and vegetables. Still dating Larry, I felt I finally had someone who truly cared for me. In September, I found out I was pregnant. When I told Larry, he said, "I will marry you but doubt I will ever love you." Sad to say he never did. A poor way to start a marriage.

We were married on October 10, 1959. Twenty minutes before I walked down the aisle, my mother-in-law-to-be told me she would have her Larry back home with her within six months. The next eleven years, she never gave up trying. We rented a house until the owner moved back, then we moved in with my parents. The day after Mother's Day, May 9, I was delivered of a beautiful baby boy with blond hair. I finally had someone I could pour out my love for and receive in return. I named him Mark David.

My folks had purchased the Vallier farm and moved into a spacious ten-room house and a barn in much better condition than the barn on the original farm. We rented the house I grew up in. Larry worked for Cloverland Electric. The first year, he worked out of town and came home on weekends. One night, I was home alone with Mark when Billy Graham came on TV in one of his crusades. That night, in front of the TV, I rededicated my life to Christ.

Our marriage wasn't the greatest. I continued being a housekeeper and cook. When Mark was about two years old, I returned to work for the state, working in the medical office of the Newberry State Hospital. My mother babysat. I worked there over a year and knew I wanted another baby. On March 25, 1963, Marsha Lynn was born. I thought I had the wrong baby. She was brown in color, and her hair was jet black and about two inches long! No wonder I had such heartburn while carrying her. She was the only baby born that day, so she had to be mine. When my Grandma Flatt saw her, she said, "She looks just like a little Korean."

It was obvious Larry had to find a job that paid more money. He was hired by Prudential Insurance. We had to move to Manistique, where he would be closer to his base in Escanaba. The move was very traumatic for Mark as he was so close to Nana and Popsie. In later years, Mark told me, "I didn't think I would ever see them again." It was when we made that move that Mark started to stutter. I wanted to get therapy for Mark, but Larry wouldn't let me, saying, "We can't afford it." We rented an apartment on Manistique Avenue, and I was a stay-at-home mom.

The year Marsha was born, all the kids in our neighborhood were getting vaccinated for measles. I took Mark and Marsha in at that time to get vaccinated. It turned out to be a bad batch of vaccine; all of the kids came down with the measles, including Mark and Marsha. Those kids were so sick for days; I held one and then the other. I didn't get much sleep. It was during a winter with lots of snow. One day, when Larry came home for lunch, I told him I had to get out of the house. I drove downtown, parked the car, and just walked down Main Street. I remember it was snowing so hard but that was all I needed. When I got back home, I was ready to hold the kids again.

We made frequent trips to the farm in Engadine, especially for a holiday when the other kids would be home. It just happened that sister-in-law Linda was pregnant when I announced that I was too, and then sister-in-law Karen announced she was pregnant too. We were all due about the same time. It seemed all three of us had complications of some sort. One time when we came home, my mother told us, "Don't you ever do this to me again." Three was too many to worry about at the same time.

Linda was the first to deliver; she had a daughter named Lisa on March 18. Twelve days later on March 30, I had Kathy Ann. Karen had Carmen on July 30. When I look back on it now, I don't know how my mother did it. We would all be home with new babies, diaper pails lined up in the utility room (that was before Pampers) and we would have baby bottles lined up on the windowsill. (that was when we still used glass bottles). We had a fun time through it all, but I'm sure my mother breathed a sigh of relief when we all left.

We saw a lot of each other when home for holidays or weddings and anniversary parties. When Marsha was about two or three, she would often disappear from the other kids and we would see her come from the utility room with a brown mouth, which meant she had gotten into the dog food again. She loved sneaking into the dog food bag.

The insurance business was not all that dependable since one worked on commission. It didn't help when you sold a good-sized policy to a business and have them cancel before you could collect your commission. Some paydays we were down to pennies in the checkbook. Larry quit that job and went to work for Frito Lay. They had excellent benefits but again beside the salary, you needed good commission.

We purchased a home on Park Avenue and lived there for about four years. In Manistique, the two main employers were the paper mill and Inland Lime & Stone. Larry was hired at Inland Lime & Stone on April 1967 when Kathy was still a baby.

Marsha often visited the lady across the street. When she came home, she would have a small bouquet of flowers picked from the lady's yard. She would give them to me. I was always so proud to get them.

Working at Inland was a seasonal job. We purchased a jeep, and Larry took many jobs in the winter plowing snow. One of the bigger jobs was plowing the parking lot of the hospital and medical center, along with numerous individual residences. We had two kids in school. My mother's health had been deteriorating. She was treated for asthma and was in the hospital being given shots and large doses of medicine that were causing severe sweating. Finally, her kidneys were shutting down. One morning when I went to see her, she told me we had to get her out of there or she would be dead.

I called my dad, told him what was going on, and by phone told the doctor to move her to the Marquette hospital. She was transported by ambulance. Upon arrival, her assigned doctor quickly took her off all medication. That was on a Tuesday. Many tests later, the doctor diagnosed her with farmer's lung. On Friday morning, I drove to Marquette to pick her up, and she *walked* through the parking lot to the car. She went to the Marshfield Clinic in Wisconsin and was on medication that seemed to put her in remission for a number of years. She was only fifty-four years old at the time.

My dad was not yet sixty-five and couldn't do all the farm work alone. My mother couldn't go near the barn because of her lung disease. Larry decided we should buy the farm and raise beef cattle. We would help my dad with the farm work for one year with him getting the milk checks. Larry would still work for Inland. I did not want to milk cows after we completely took over the farm. My folks purchased a mobile home and placed it on the other side of the apple orchard on an acre of land. We had only been moved three months when Larry announced he wanted to milk cows. I never wanted to milk another cow ever again. Larry won out. My dad helped with the chores, and after another year Larry quit working at Inland so we could become full-time dairy farmers.

We had lived in Manistique nine years. The year we moved to the farm Kathy started school; now all three kids were in school. My dad started working at the golf course at the Hiawatha Club. He loved the job and worked there for many years. He finally retired at the age of eighty-seven. At that time, he was the oldest man in Michigan to be drawing an unemployment check. As time went on, we built onto the barn, put up a metal building that held our equipment, and built a garage. We went from Grade B to Grade A milk, which required a milk house with a big bulk tank for the milk.

By then Mark had moved to Colorado Springs. There he learned carpenter work from Ron Schroeder, who built Martin Homes. Marsha enrolled at Western in Kalamazoo, and Kathy was in high school.

One spring, Mark came home from Colorado, and we were getting fields ready to plant. The whole family was out in a forty-acre field picking stones and hauling them to the stone pile. When we came back to the house for lunch, there on the back porch was a vase with a dozen red roses. Mark had gotten them for me for Mother's Day. When I read the card, I cried and cried, and Mark asked, "What's wrong, Mom? They are supposed to make you happy." I told him they were the first flowers I had ever received. He then proceeded to tell me that as long as we were both alive, I would be receiving flowers from him for every Mother's Day. I was in my thirties then. He has kept his promise. I get flowers from him every Mother's Day, and I am weeks away from my eighty-third birthday.

During our early farming years, I was getting B12 injections for neuritis in my right jaw. I had been getting one shot a month for about six years. This one particular day, my mom drove to Manistique and I went with her. While there, I told her I needed a shot, so she took me to the clinic. I went in, the nurse gave me the usual injection, I left (not waiting the twenty minutes), and we headed for home. We were less than halfway home when I was hit with a drug reaction.

My life stood still. I could not move my body at all, and my whole life flashed before me from the present to when I was a little girl. My mother noticed something that made her ask if I was all right. I managed to say, "Help me." She turned the car around and headed back to the clinic. There was road construction, and traffic was backed up. A state police car was parked off to the side. Mom pulled up to him, honking the horn, and screamed, "Medical emergency!" Lights came on, with the siren going, and we were on our way.

By the time I got there, I could move. I was able to walk into the clinic staggering, and a nurse grabbed me and got me into a room while another nurse ran for the doctor. For the next two hours, Dr. Larry Sell never left my side. He gave me an injection with a huge needle, and three different times I was walking through a tunnel with a bright light at the end of the tunnel. Just before I would get to the end, something grabbed the back of my shirt and pulled me back. Each time I was praying, "Lord, don't let me die. I have three young kids to raise."

Once I was stabilized, I was admitted to the hospital. I remained there three days. During that time, I neither got a call nor a visit from Larry. When it was time to go home, I called my mother to pick me up.

For entertainment, the VFW held dances most Saturday nights with local music. We went to those dances most weekends. Larry and I got along all right, but true to his word he never loved me. We worked well together but I was his cook and housekeeper.

Mark and Marsha were home for Christmas and New Year's. That New Year's Eve, Larry and I drove to the VFW hall for the annual dance held there. Something happened from the time we left home until we arrived at the hall in that three-mile stretch. Larry refused to be near me. If I sat next to him, he would get up and sit with other people. That kept up all evening. Before midnight, I finally said I wanted to go home because it was obvious he didn't want to be near me. We started for home, and about halfway there he stopped the truck. Glaring at me, he called me horrid names and told me he wanted a divorce. To this day, I don't know what caused the apparent chemical change, but it never left. I felt like I had been kicked in the gut.

I went to bed, and he paced the floor like a caged lion. At some point, he stood over the bed and repeated the same vile words as he did in the truck. It was the beginning of a six-year nightmare. Not one word was spoken between us for the next three days, and even the cows would turn their heads looking at us, wondering what was wrong. The third day while in the barn, he threw me against the wall and said he shouldn't have said what he did. Nothing was ever the same after that.

Mark returned to Colorado, and Marsha went back to college with Kathy attending high school.

During those years, interest was quite high, so we were able to save enough money to pay cash for new equipment. We sold all the bull calves to a beef farmer in McMillan. We had a heifer about to have her first calf on a Sunday afternoon in a field near the house. She was having problems, and after an allotted time, we pulled the calf. The calf's tongue was hanging out, blue in color, and looked like it was dead. After watching it for a few seconds, I saw it blink an eye. I opened the little one's mouth, took out all the mucus I could, and started CPR. It didn't take long before I had worked up a sweat since it was in the summer. I just kept up the CPR, and before long he let out a "bah." I was so proud of him. I wiped him down, getting the circulation going. The money from that calf went to me. Then the price of milk bottomed out, and so did the price for our bull calves.

On one occasion, I had just returned home from driving Marsha back to college, which made for a very long day. My cousin had driven with me so I wouldn't get sleepy on the way home. I arrived at 1:00 a.m. when Larry told me a good friend, Edwin Nichols, died of a heart attack. We went to the funeral home for the wake. There I saw Richard Hammermeister, standing off to the side. I went up to him saying hello, and he didn't recognize me. I told him who I was, and he proceeded to give me a big bear hug saying, "It's been so many years," to which I replied, "Yes, thirty-one years." He introduced me to his wife. We didn't spend much time talking.

The following morning was the funeral. Larry was in one of his sarcastic depressive moods and refused to go to the funeral. After the funeral, a lunch was served in the basement. After we had eaten, Rich approached me, and we exchanged news of what had transpired in the last thirty-one years. He asked me if I had a happy marriage; I lied and told him I did. He proceeded to tell me he was on the verge of a separation. Before I left for home, he gave me a phone number and said, "If you ever need me for help, this is the number to call." I thanked him and left.

Several times after that, he and Edna visited with my uncle or his aunt and would stop by. Once we had them over for dinner. Soon after, Rich was separated from his wife and was living with a friend. I had the phone number tucked away in my billfold. It remained there for the next four and a half years.

One morning, I woke up and could hardly lift my left arm, and my shoulder really hurt. I had not hurt it in any way so I couldn't understand the pain I was feeling. Later that day, Mark called from Colorado saying he had been in a car accident; he had whiplash and had hurt his left shoulder. I then knew why I had the pain in my left shoulder all day. The next day, my arm and shoulder were fine.

The price of milk had dropped, and the bull calves were not paying enough. We decided to sell the cows and machinery. At that time, a lot of farmers were getting rid of their herds. If we sold our cows, we were not allowed to sell any individually to anyone, which was sad because we had some very good milkers that my cousin next door would have bought. The cows had to be sold as a lot. They had to go to a slaughterhouse downstate which took several hours' travel time. I called the auction place and asked them to sell our herd first since they were good milkers and would be dripping milk like crazy.

Larry went with Jack Gribbell, who trucked our cows to slaughter. What a sad day that was. It was summer, and I asked Kathy to go with me to be gone for the day. We spent the day in another town and had lunch there. We put up FOR SALE signs and lined up the machinery. We had no problem selling it because everyone knew we kept the machinery inside during winter and it was all in excellent shape.

Larry had a brother, Arne, living in Pennsylvania. I asked Larry if he thought things could improve between us if we moved near his brother and away from all of my relatives. He thought it would be a good move and we could find work there. Kathy had graduated from high school as salutatorian of her class and moved to Pennsylvania, living with her Uncle Arne and Aunt Blanche. She worked in an office at Lomont Farms, which raised racehorses.

Back in Michigan, we held a huge garage sale and sold almost everything. The farm was for sale. The evening of sale day, we received a call from a woman who had been to our sale; she wanted to know if she and her husband could come and look at the farm. They came, looked, and bought the farm! We didn't have to put it in the hands of a realtor. In August, we drove to York Pennsylvania and purchased a house, paying cash for it. In September, Kathy flew to Miami, Florida, where she went for intense training at a school for a month. Marsha quit her job in Kalamazoo, moved to PA when we did, and obtained a very good job at the Bon-Ton department store. Kathy finished her schooling, came back to PA, and went to work for AAA. Both girls lived with us.

Two weeks after we moved to Pennsylvania, Larry once again told me to pack up and get out. He wanted a divorce. We had just purchased new furniture for the house. I told him he could leave if he wanted to, but I was staying. The next six months were a nightmare. I never knew what might happen. I kept begging him to seek help, but he refused. Larry found a job at a garage and worked from 11:00 a.m. to 6:00 p.m. He was paid very well. I did some sewing for the girls.

That Christmas, Mark came home from Colorado, and I knew it would be the last time we would all be together as a family. I would sit in my chair, enjoying the fire in the fireplace and wondering what the future held and where would I be a year from now. About four months later, I moved the girls to an apartment so they would be farther away, knowing if something happened to me, they would be safe.

One day when Larry left for work, I got the Bible out. I looked up scriptures and I prayed hard all day. I made a promise to God that if *he* could get me away from there, I would let *him* guide me the rest of my life. Nothing is stronger than the power of prayer. I gave my life to Christ many years before and didn't rely on *him* like I should have until that day.

The next day, I got my answer. I was still in touch with Rich. That day, after four and a half years, I called him and told him I needed help. He was just recovering from a TIA. He told me he had a friend in South Carolina or Texas that might help. I chose Texas. He called his friend and made arrangements for the move. He also needed doctoring at Wilford Hall in San Antonio where the Michigan doctor was sending him for more tests. Rich was retired from the Army with twenty years of service.

The hardest thing I ever had to do in my life was to say goodbye to my girls and not let them know I was leaving. In April 1986, Rich came to Pennsylvania, where I loaded some things in his pickup and packed my Dodge Charger. I left Larry's signed paycheck, my credit cards, and the checkbook all lying on the kitchen counter. Rich and I struck out for Texas. I was a mental mess leaving my girls behind. Lots of tears were shed on my drive to Texas. I called them every night to make sure they were all right. The whole trip to Texas was very traumatic for me because I left my girls with uncertainty of what might happen to them.

Two and a half days later, we arrived in San Antonio. Rich called Ed, and Ed told him where to go to spend the night. Ed and Linda met us at the motel, and the next day, they both took off a day from work and helped us find an apartment. We rented furniture. The following morning, Rich and I went our separate ways looking for work. Rich was hired right away at a 7-Eleven station and store. I put my application in at three different department stores at Ingram Mall, which was about six miles from our apartment.

Three days later, I was called by JCPenney's for an interview. I was hired and started training the next day. There were about ten of us in training. After we had eaten lunch and were waiting for the instructor to come back, Christine Walker asked each of us when we had put in our application and how long it was before we were called for an interview. Most of them had waited six months to a year.

When it came my turn, I told them I applied on Thursday and was called on Monday for an interview. Christine said to me "Girl, the Good Lord sure is looking after you." To which I replied, "Chris, you will never know how much." That was the start of my forty-four-year friendship with my Black friend, Chris, whom I love very much. Our friendship is still ongoing. She is the best friend I ever had.

About one week into my new job, I had a dream. It was the first of many dreams guiding my life. In the dream, I was dressed in jeans, a white blouse, and white tennis shoes. No gloves. I started climbing a very high, rocky, mountain-like wall. I had to grip the sharp rocks as I climbed. When I reached the top, I pulled myself over the flat surface and stood up on beautiful green grass. As I turned a complete circle, it was as though I saw the whole world. Trees, mountains, water, and plains. I looked at my hands; they were not dirty or bleeding from the climb. My blouse was still snow white; I wasn't tired. I knew I would be safe and could start a whole new life.

My daughter Kathy was working for AAA. One day about a month after I moved, Kathy asked me in conversation how much I had to pay for my new state registration for my car. Without hesitating, I told her the amount and all she said was "Oh." When I asked her why she wanted to know, she gave me a flimsy excuse, which I fell for. The next time we talked, she told me she knew where I was.

I said to her, "You think you know where I am."

She replied "No, I know where you are." She proceeded to explain to me, and I was speechless. All I could say was "You little shit." She had looked up the registration where she worked. What a detective I had in the family. All through her life, she has been a detective in one way or another and I always told her she should get a job with the FBI. It is still a joke between us.

I had to wait six months to apply for a divorce because I had moved from another state. At Penney's, I worked all the hours I could get and three months after I started working there, I asked for five days off so I could fly to Pennsylvania and move my daughter to San Antonio. They told me I hadn't been there long enough to get time off. I proceeded to tell them I had to have the time off even if it meant I lost my job. They gave me the five days off. Once again, God's grace.

I could hardly wait to see the girls again. When I got to the Baltimore airport, both girls were waiting for me. The three of us hugged and cried for what seemed an eternity. There was a woman standing behind the girls, waiting for someone to get off the plane. She kept watching us, and before I knew it, she was crying as hard as we were. We drove to the girl's apartment. Kathy and I both liked Garfield the cat, and I had given her a standing Garfield figurine, which stood quite tall. When I walked in the door, Garfield was standing in a corner. Kathy said he had been bad that day. All three of us had a hearty laugh for the first time in months.

The next day, Kathy and I would be leaving for Texas in her car. Marsha was going to go back to Michigan with her dad; the girls' furniture was packed in a van and sent to Texas for Kathy. It was very hot that summer, and Kathy had no air conditioning in her car. I had a cooler packed with ice water and a washcloth to keep wiping my face with to keep cool. I used it; Kathy didn't. We drove to Lafayette, Louisiana, to stop for something to drink. As we walked into McDonald's, Kathy started sweating profusely with water running down her legs and arms. We got to the counter, and with the AC being quite cool, she passed out over the counter. A man behind me helped me get her in a booth. She came to; I purchased drinks to go, got her into the car, and headed across the street to a motel. I got her into bed and started sponging her. The TV was on; on the screen, they showed the seven signs of heatstroke. Kathy said, "Look, Mom, I have all seven."

She was better by morning, and we were on the road again by 4:30 a.m. I ended up driving the rest of the way to San Antonio as Kathy was too sick to drive. We arrived at our apartment early afternoon. There was Rich sitting by the table with two bouquets of flowers, one for Kathy and one for me. Kathy had a hard time adjusting to my living with Rich.

I went back to work at Penney's, but I was only getting twenty-eight hours a week. Not enough to live on. We found an apartment for Kathy. The moving van arrived from Pennsylvania with her furniture. Kathy started looking for work, putting her application in at many places. She was hired by Southwest Airlines within a couple of weeks.

The new life in Texas certainly was different. I had always thought of Texas like I saw in the movies. All sand, cactus, and cowboys. The eastern part was green, hilly, with lots of longhorn beef. I remember stopping at a rest area, sitting by a picnic table and just watching the longhorns eating in the pasture. Houston was so big. Arriving in San Antonio was a whole new way of life.

Penney's kept shortening my hours, and Rich was looking for a better job that would offer benefits. Rich applied at the Audie Murphy VA Hospital and was called to work shortly after he applied. We began looking for a house to buy and found one on Cedarbend, not far from where my friend Chris, my colleague at Penney's, lived. In the meantime, a customer came into Penney's and in conversation I told her I was looking for another job with more hours. She told me her husband was an optometrist at another mall and was looking for a contact lens technician. She told me to put my application in at Texas State Optical where her husband worked, and it would be on-the-job training. I was hired and gave my two weeks' notice to Penney's. Both Rich and I had better jobs and Kathy was doing well at Southwest.

About that time, I found out from one of the women I worked with that a class in sign language was being taught at Cornerstone Church. Rich and I were both interested in learning sign language and we signed up for the class. When we were near the end of the class, each student was asked to sign a song and not speak a word while doing it. Rich had picked "Onward Christian Soldiers" and breezed through it, and the whole class understood. I guess I was too confident, wanting to sign "How Great Thou Art." When my turn came to sign, I drew a blank. I never did live that one down.

We moved into our new home on Cedarbend, and again I was looking for another job that had more benefits. I enrolled in a business school, learning how to use a computer. I had never seen a computer before then. I enrolled in classes from 5:30 p.m. to 10:00 p.m. and studied three different classes. I was about forty-eight years old by then, and all of the other students were fresh out of high school. I was the grandma of the class. You graduated according to how fast you completed each course. There were about fifteen students in the class. I told Kathy and Rich I was going to be the first one to graduate and with straight A's. That is just what I did.

The year my granddaughter Leah Lynn was born, May 20, 1992, all three of the kids said they would like to spend Christmas with Rich and me. Marsha lived in Michigan, Mark in Colorado Springs, and Kathy in San Antonio. All three married mates who had been divorced and each had a sibling. The combined families with the step-grandchildren numbered ten. Marsha caught the twenty-four-hour flu on the plane; needless to say, it went through all twelve of us in two days. We were glad we had two bathrooms and lots of wastebaskets.

Marsha wanted Leah to be baptized at our church during that time. I told her I would like to make her christening gown. Kathy had saved my wedding gown and brought it to Texas with her. I cut the satin skirt off the gown and cut out the christening gown. It was one of the bigger challenges I have ever undertaken. When it was finished, I said, "Bonnie Prince Charles's gown wasn't any nicer than the one I made." Granddaughter Jordan was baptized in it the following year. Years later, Leah's brother, Andrew, was baptized wearing it. In March 2019, Leah's daughter Emma Jane wore it. I wanted to embroider their names on the bottom of the dress but never got around to it.

Texas required a six-month waiting period to apply for an out-of-state divorce. Having moved to Texas in April, I had to wait until September to apply for a divorce. It became final in December 1986. We set the date of our wedding for Valentine's Day, 1987. It was sixty-seven degrees that day with some rain. Ed and Linda stood up for our wedding, and Kathy gave me away. We each wrote our own wedding vows. We were married at the Lutheran church we attended. Our pastor was in the Holy Land at the time, so the chaplain from Lackland Air Force Base married us.

My marriage to Rich was a good one, and I finally became a wife besides cook and housekeeper.

Rich had been a member of the Fraternal Order of Eagles back in Michigan and had his membership transferred. I joined the Eagles in the fall of 1987. We went to most activities there and we also loved to play bingo at the American Legion, where we were members. We did a little traveling and one of the trips was to Desert Hot Springs, CA, where we visited an aunt. Rich was an alcoholic. We attended a lot of parties, and I would drink right along with Rich. By the time we left San Antonio, I could really pack it away. I'm not proud of those years of drinking. That was to change eventually.

Many times, Rich would call from work at the hospital saying he would be home later because he would be sitting with a patient who was waiting for their family to come from Corpus Christi or another town. He would sit and hold their hand and just be there to listen to what they had to say or just sit in silence until the family members arrived. The waiting period was more pronounced when San Antonio was hit with a tornado that did a lot of damage to the hospital.

One time in particular, Rich called me at work and wanted to know if we had homemade chicken noodle soup in the freezer. I told him we did, and he promptly hung up. When he came home from work, he told me there was a man in his early thirties dying of AIDS. He had just days left to live. While Rich was cleaning his room, the man had said to Rich, "I would give anything for a bowl of home-made chicken noodle soup." Rich asked the nurses if it would be all right to bring him some soup and they said, "No problem." The next morning, Rich brought the chicken noodle soup to work, the nurses warmed it up, and he had it for breakfast. He passed away two days later.

Some of the patients who were well enough worked in a craft room. One of the male patients who was in cancer treatment asked Rich what my name was and how to spell it; he wanted to make something out of wood. He carved the name "Shirley" in writing, not printing, making me a nameplate for my desk at work. It was beautiful. All these years later, it is still sitting on top of our maple rolltop desk.

Chapter
3

In the nine years we lived in San Antonio, we spent seven Septembers of the nine in Michigan. My mother's pulmonary fibrosis was getting worse, and it seemed every September she would end up in the hospital. She was given medication, but it didn't help because of the type of fibrosis she had. All of us kids were home once when she was in the hospital and once again, she pulled through and was able to go home.

I started applying for office jobs that required a computer. All the while, I was afraid I might not be able to handle an office job. One afternoon, I was walking through the mall and walked into a bookstore. I went to the religious section, not looking for anything in particular. There, standing on a shelf about eye-level was a book by Norman Vincent Peale called *You Can If You Think You Can*. Thank you, Lord. You gave me the answer. I bought the book, read it, and never doubted job offers again. Once again, God was guiding me.

I had a couple of different jobs doing computer work, and then I was offered a full-time job with Blue Cross Blue Shield. The training took about three weeks. It was during that time that Marsha and John were married in Sault Ste. Marie, Michigan, on July 14, 1989. We were unable to attend the wedding because of my training classes.

Working there was an experience. The supervisor paced up and down the aisle, watching each one of us in our little cubicle, with her hands behind her back. She made you feel like she was a prison warden and we were in a prison. Thankfully, I was called for jury duty, and the trial lasted six weeks. I collected wages from Blue Cross Blue

Shield for the entire duration of the trial. If we were dismissed early on a trial day, I was out putting my application in for another job. A week before the trial ended, I found another job. When I went back to BCBS to pick up my things, I found out that seven other women had quit that same week. Turnover was very heavy at that office.

Suzie was willing to have "temp help" until the trial ended so I could start working there. It was an interesting job as the company made molds for CorningWare. The sand needed for making the molds was trucked into San Antonio all the way from Boyne Falls, Michigan, because of certain mineral in the sand. Four months into that job, the "main man" flew in on his private plane from Dallas and announced that the last 25 percent of the people hired would no longer be working there as of 5:00 p.m. that night. I was told about it at 4:50 p.m. Since I was the last one hired, I lost my job before it really began. When I told my mother-in-law I had lost my job, without hesitation she said, "God never closes a door without opening a window."

It didn't take long after searching the want ads that I found a job as office manager at a psychotherapy office working for five therapists. It was a very depressing job with some days more depressing than others. On those days, I would change clothes after work and run on the college track across the street. Sometimes I would walk, and other times run, depending on how the day went. By the time I would get back to the car, I was relaxed enough to leave work behind me. It became too stressful for me, so when I made my last car payment, I gave notice that I was quitting.

My next and final job in San Antonio was with an insurance company where I worked for almost four years. Once again, I could use my computer skills, being a typist for one of many adjusters working there. I really liked the work, and it had good benefits and medical coverage. About that time, gangs were more prevalent in the city, and drive-by shootings were happening several times a week.

During the years spent in San Antonio, both Rich and I were active in craft shows. He made three wind chimes in different sizes and also made fishing sinkers. Most of the fishing sinkers were sold to employees at the hospital. I painted T-shirts and sweatshirts, made fleece blankets, and a lot more items. The wind chimes were a big item to sell as many people bought them for gifts for "people who have everything; what do you buy them?" We had quite a production line in putting them together. We would lay out the three sizes on the floor in the living room, and with tools in hand, one would hold and the other would string or clamp. In this way we could complete a set in fifteen minutes. We had them in five different countries and at least twenty-five states.

We had a beautiful patio at the back of our home. I had a lot of hanging plants as well as pots on the floor. We ate at our picnic table a lot and would spend hours watching cloud formations in the big Texas sky. There were a lot of rosebushes in our backyard, and we also had a garden where we grew tomatoes, green peppers, onions, and green beans.

While I was working for the insurance company one summer, my brother-in-law in Michigan passed away from cancer. Rich and I flew home for the funeral. I was to have my first encounter with my ex-husband. Six years had passed since our divorce, and I was very bitter and actually felt a hate toward him for what he had done to the kids and me. My brother and I were standing in front of the casket talking when Larry walked in. The minute he saw me, he started crying very hard. When I saw what was happening, I could feel all the hate I had harbored against him drain from my body. Instead I felt sorry for him. We were to run into each other several times after that, but he refused to talk to me. I would not have had a problem with at least saying hello especially if any of our kids were around.

My daughter Kathy married Scott on July 28, 1992, in Las Vegas. Scott was raised in San Antonio, and Kathy had met him through one of the women she worked with at Southwest Airlines. Less than a month later, Rich and I flew to Colorado Springs where my son Mark married Eva in a beautiful ceremony on August 21. Mark was the only one of my children that I got to see get married.

The following June, I received a call in the early morning that Kathy was about to deliver. I called work to let them know I wouldn't be in that day. It always amazed me when being on the farm I witnessed the birth of a new baby calf and what a miracle it was. That was nothing compared to being in the delivery room and witnessing the birth of my granddaughter, Jordan, on that June 11 morning. To see her get slapped on the butt, hear that first cry, and know that she had ten fingers and ten toes. How precious life is and what a miracle birth is. The following year my grandson Eric was born in Colorado Springs on June 3. I now had three grandchildren and three step-grandchildren. I love them all very much.

Rich and I decided it was time to move on. We decided to move to Colorado Springs, Colorado, where my son Mark lived. Rich never had children of his own, so he enjoyed mine. We found a place to rent in Colorado Springs and we both gave our two weeks' notice in Texas that we were moving. Rich retired from Audie Murphy VA hospital. The following Sunday, we attended Palm Sunday Service at Oak Hills Church of Christ where Max Lucado was and still is pastor. I felt so honored to have attended church services at Chrystal Cathedral with Robert Schueller in California, Cornerstone with John Hagee, and Oak Hills Church of Christ with Max Lucado in San Antonio. After Easter, we were on our way to Colorado Springs.

Within two weeks of our move, I received a phone call from one of the women I worked with at the insurance company. She told me the insurance company was moving to North Carolina, and if anyone wanted to keep working for the company, they would have to move to North Carolina. If they chose not to move, they would have to look for employment elsewhere. I had left just in time.

Once we were in Colorado, I started the task of looking for work. I did temp work at several medical offices, doctor's offices, and attorney's offices. I worked with a very nice lady named Lynn at one of the medical offices. She was from New York. We spent a lot of time together, sharing our past, discussing the present, and also what we hoped for in the future. God played a big part in our conversations. She found employment at an attorney's office a couple of months later, and we lost contact. I had given her a name card of mine before she left.

God has our lives so planned out and we don't realize at the time how *he* puts certain people and things in our life. After living in an apartment for six months, we started looking for a house to buy. Our home in San Antonio was on the market but the market was very slow. Our lease was about to run out on the apartment. About that time, Rich was summoned to Michigan to help find a nursing home for his mother. I found a nice trilevel home, and after much faxing of paperwork and details of the home back and forth to Detroit, Rich decided he liked it. We bought it and moved in that fall.

I was content working in medical offices and clinics but wanted something more permanent. Late one afternoon, I was unpacking a box and a small piece of paper fell out. It was advertising a correspondence course in medical transcription from a company in Georgia. I called the number and signed up for the course. It was designed so that you worked at your own pace. You could call them to get the results of a test you had taken. When I called for the results of the last test, I was informed that I was only the second person to ever pass the test on the first try—and at a score of 91! It had been a hard one, and I had worked on it for over a week before submitting it. After nine months, I received my certificate as a medical transcriptionist. I finished the course with straight A's.

Once again God intervened in my life. A woman was advertising for a transcriptionist to help in a pediatric clinic. I went to her house, and during the interview discovered she was from Traverse City, Michigan. I told her I was from the Upper Peninsula of Michigan. We hit it off, and thus I became one of five transcriptionists working for her. We got paid by the line. In high school, I never typed more than 55 wpm but doing transcription I was up to 80 wpm. I also became her courier. I would pick up and deliver the transcription the next day.

On one occasion, while on my pickup run, I was driving on I-25. It was winter, the sun was setting behind Pikes Peak, and I saw the two biggest sun dogs I had ever seen. The rainbow colors were so vibrant that I pulled off the highway and just sat there taking it all in. What beauty only God could display.

Typing the transcription was a fascinating job, and I learned a lot. One day, we were transcribing for another office besides the pediatric clinic. For years I had been doctoring with specialists to find out what the problem was with my right ear. This one particular case I was typing was of a woman describing her ear problem, and it was exactly what I had been experiencing. The final diagnosis was a dysfunctional eustachian tube. After all the money and years I had spent only to be told, "I can't find anything wrong," I finally got the diagnosis while transcribing!

During our years in Colorado Springs, Rich kept busy making different crafts. We would spend a lot of time at Home Depot looking for lumber with no knots for the angels Rich made. I would help him assemble the angels and other woodcrafts and then finish them with varnish and whatever else was needed. We attended lots of craft shows.

The church we attended in Colorado Springs had an interpreter for the deaf. We became acquainted with a couple who sat in the deaf section. By sitting in the deaf section, we could keep up with the little we had learned in sign language class in Texas. John was a hearing person, but his wife was not. She had lost her hearing at an early age but was good at lip-reading. About a year later, her husband was in the hospital for surgery and we met the pastor from Denver who did the signing for the doctor in translation. We became friends with the pastor and his wife and were invited to church functions with the deaf.

Our last year in Colorado, the Denver pastor's father-in-law passed away in Kansas. We were supposed to have our Christmas party in Castle Rock, and suddenly she had to leave. She asked me to take her place. What a challenge. I had no problem fixing the meal, and I had the gifts made for all the women in attendance. What scared me to death was how I would communicate with the women since I knew very little sign language. The pastor assured me I would be fine. The women were very patient and helpful with conversation. If I made an incorrect sign, they would have a big smile, shake their head no, and show me the correct sign. It was so funny, we all ended up laughing, and it certainly put me at ease. They were a great group of women, and I have thought of them often since we moved from Colorado.

Once in a while, we need a reminder that what is considered permanent and definite is merely a limitation we set. We sometimes forget God is in charge, and that with faith and love, anything is possible. God's gifts are large and small, long and short. I thank *him* for the precious miracle moments he gave me in 1997.

When I married for the second time in 1987, I not only married the man I had dated thirty-six years before but I also inherited a wonderful mother-in-law named Helen. Right from the start, I was treated like her daughter, and I grew to love her very much. She lived in South Rockwood, Michigan. We were living in San Antonio at the time and because of our work, we were not able to visit her as often as we would have liked. So we would call Mom, and her first words were always "Oh, for goodness's sake, what a surprise."

We managed to fly to Michigan at least once a year. Mom lived on a farm and in the mornings, we would sit on the beloved wooden swing in her backyard, drink coffee, and watch the robins and rabbits run around the big backyard going to the barn. In the evening, we would watch the sunshine on the old yet sturdy barn and capture the copper colors of the rusty metal roof. Gently the sun disappeared behind the building that symbolized years of hard work, togetherness as a family, and a love of the outdoors. We saw many beautiful sunsets, and Mom would say, "Shirley, isn't that one of the most beautiful sunsets you have ever seen?"

On May 1, 1995, Rich and I moved to Colorado Springs, and our phone conversations with Mom became limited. By September 1995, Mom's Alzheimer's became much worse, and she was placed in a nursing home. When we called, she had a hard time remembering who we were.

In July of 1996, we drove to Michigan. The first day we saw Mom at the nursing home, she knew who we were. We had a very nice visit and talked again about how we would sit in the backyard and watch the robins in the morning and sunsets at night. The second day of our visit, she did not know who we were. Alzheimer's is a very cruel disease. We returned to Colorado, and that was the last time we saw Mom alive. When we would call the nursing home to check on her, we were only able to talk to the nurses. They would give us an update on her physical and mental health. Her main dream was to go home. She lived for the day she could move back into her farmhouse.

When friends and family visited, she often didn't know who they were. Our hearts ached knowing she was confused and unhappy. We felt helpless to provide comfort.

Sunday morning, February 22, 1997, we called the nursing home to see how Mom was doing. The nurse who answered the phone said, "I just left Helen's room. Let me get her for you." It seemed only seconds until Mom said hello. We said, "Hi, Mom," and she said, "Oh, for goodness's sake. What a surprise. I'm so glad you called."

We had a very pleasant conversation. Mom's mind was as clear as can be. She asked about Colorado and told us she was not feeling well, was very tired, and that her cold was getting worse. She stated four times how she wanted to go home. As our conversation ended, she said, "I feel better already. I love you both."

Two and a half weeks later, we received a call around midnight from the nursing home saying Mom was very sick and was being rushed to the hospital. She had developed pneumonia and had an obstructed bowel. They were forced to operate. Mom lived four days after surgery and passed away on March 16.

When we arrived at the funeral home, we talked to Donna, a sister-in-law, who told us that for the past month Mom did not know anyone. Donna would visit her twice a week, and Mom would say "Who did you say you are?" The last days of Mom's life, Donna visited twice a day reading to her from the Bible or *Portals of Prayer*. Mom didn't know who she was. The pastor told us he was unable to give her communion the last month of her life because of her confusion. We told the pastor of our last conversation with her just two and a half weeks before, and he was very surprised. We told him how each time we called the nursing home, we talked with a nurse but this last time we spoke to Mom, and her mind was as it was many years ago. I told him I felt God had cleared her mind for one last conversation with us, and he agreed.

The day of the funeral was the first day of spring. Robins were enjoying the yard. The temperature broke a record, reaching seventy-five degrees. Mom was laid to rest next to Dad, under a big tree with a small set of wind chimes on one of the tree limbs blowing in the breeze. That evening, sitting on the cherished wooden swing, Rich and I witnessed a spectacular sunset, and the simple yet awesome routine of another day fading behind the barn. It was as if we could feel Mom looking down on us and saying, "Kids, isn't this one of the most beautiful sunsets you've ever seen?" At last Mom was *home*.

As time went on, both Rich and I were having problems with altitude sickness. It was either bad headaches or flulike symptoms near constantly. One day after delivering the transcription, Kim and I took time to talk about home, missing the fall colors of maple and various trees in Michigan. That same day while I was transcribing, my son Mark called. He *never* called me during working hours. As we talked, I told him about Kim and I talking about Michigan. Mark said, "I don't want to sound like I am trying to get rid of you, but why don't you and Rich move back to Michigan where you can be healthy again?"

I told Rich about both conversations. That Sunday morning, while eating breakfast, we were listening to a sermon by Robert Schuller. During his sermon, he talked about God giving us signs which we don't always recognize. He said, "Sometimes God puts you in touch with a friend, a relative, a sermon, or even a letter which can transform your life." I had the friend, Kim; the relative, Mark; and now the sermon. I told Rich, "If I receive a letter within the next five days that is unusual, it is our sign to move back to Michigan."

Two days later, I was in my office transcribing, and Rich brought the mail in. All of a sudden, he said, "Put your work on save and come up here right now." I had received a letter from Lynn, the woman I had worked with at a medical clinic over a year and a half before. She was going through some papers and found my name card I had given her. She was checking to see if I ever took the course in transcription and how I was doing. She referred to me as her guardian angel and said she had moved back to New York. When I finished reading the letter, Rich said, "When do we move?" Once again, divine intervention.

In January, we put the house up for sale thinking it could be months before we would have a buyer. Two weeks later, the buyer was at our house. He bought it for his daughter but didn't need it until March. That was fine with us. In the meantime, we decided to move to Grayling, Michigan. I subscribed to their newspaper and started looking for a place to rent. Nothing was available, and then two weeks before we were to move, we got a call saying he had an apartment available. He not only had the apartment but told us he had an empty garage we could store our furniture in until we found a home and there would be no added cost for the garage space. Is God great or what!

March 1997 we headed back to Michigan. It was a very cold winter. We arrived in Grayling, Michigan, on a Saturday afternoon, and the temperature was negative twenty-two degrees below zero. The next afternoon, we went to the Fraternal Order of Eagles to get acquainted with people and ask questions like where we could find a good hairdresser, where to bank, etc. Tending the bar was a striking lady with a great personality. She gave us a lot of help, and thus a great friendship started between Christine Oswald and me. There is a saying that we are blessed if in our lifetime we can have one very good friend for life. I was blessed with two. I have Christine Walker in San Antonio and Christine Oswald in Grayling. How blessed can you be?

Rich did a lot of fishing in the summer as we had two lakes close by. I hadn't had any luck finding a job, so I started working as a volunteer at the Grayling hospital. I worked 6:00 a.m. to 1:30 p.m. at the outpatient nurses' station. Once again, I learned a lot from the doctors' dictating.

One day, while speaking with one of the sisters who ran the Battered Women's Shelter, I asked if it would be all right to possibly bake a birthday cake for a woman or child who would have a birthday while staying at the shelter. She checked with the other sisters and called to tell me I would be allowed to bake birthday cakes. They would call me with a first name and age of the woman or child, and I would decorate the cake accordingly. I would deliver the cake to the door, never seeing the person the cake was for.

One day, I received a phone call from the shelter telling me about a twenty-five-year-old woman I had baked a cake for. When the sisters gave her the cake, they said she cried and cried. When they asked her why she was crying, she told them it was the first birthday cake she ever had in her life, and it came from a stranger. I baked many more cakes before and after that during the four years I worked at the hospital. Each time I delivered a cake, I thanked God for making someone's birthday a little better under not-so-happy times in their lives.

While still in Grayling, we would drive to the UP to see my parents quite often. My mother's idiopathic pulmonary fibrosis was really taking a toll on her. Her cough was worse, and everything was slowing down.

Labor Day weekend 1998, all of us kids were home, and we had a combined birthday party for both Mom and Popsie. She turned eighty on August 28, and Popsie would be ninety on October 11. Two of Popsie's brothers were there and two sisters and a brother of my Mom's, plus grandkids and a couple of friends. It was a nice party, but little did we know my dad had just weeks to live. Within two weeks, my mother was on full-time oxygen.

Popsie was so dedicated to taking care of Mom that he neglected his own health. On September 29, 1998, around midnight, Rich and I received a call informing us that my dad was hemorrhaging and was being rushed to the Marquette Hospital from the Newberry Hospital. They almost lost him on the way there. He ended up needing stomach surgery. He seemed to be doing all right. All but one of us kids was there; the youngest son, Gary, was in Alaska at the time.

Rich and I stayed in the hospital's hospitality room, as did my mother. We would hook up her oxygen tank to the back of her wheelchair, and I would push her into Popsie's room where she would spend most of the day. That went on for eight days. The ninth day there, Popsie started to hemorrhage, and his health was deteriorating fast. Members of the family spent the night with him, and each had a chance to speak to him alone. Saturday it was obvious Popsie was losing his battle. Numerous tests were done but there was not anything left for the doctors to try. All we could do was pray. I remember standing in the hallway outside of his room and praying,

"Lord, please let him live till midnight so he can make his ninetieth birthday."

Saturday night, my brother Gary, who lived in Washington State, was able to fly to Green Bay, Wisconsin, and drove to the hospital. He arrived around midnight and spent several hours alone with Popsie. Then arrived Sunday morning, October 11, my dad's ninetieth birthday.

About 6:00 a.m., Rich went to check at the nurses' station while I was in the shower. Rich came back and said, "Hurry and get dressed. Popsie is hemorrhaging." He woke my mother while I quickly dressed and ran a comb through my wet hair. I wheeled my Mom into his room, and as we entered the room, Popsie had the strangest, contented look on his face. Looking at my mother, he said, "Jesus is waiting for me." Mom just looked at him, not knowing what to say. Then he said to me, "I tried so hard to get better so I could take care of Mom."

I replied, "I know you did, but Jesus has other plans for you. Don't worry. We will take care of Mom."

He replied, "I know you will."

The hemorrhaging continued. Mom was in the waiting room with most of the other siblings. Being Sunday, a local pastor from the college came to see my dad. My dad asked me to stay by his side while the pastor prayed. He told the pastor he was not afraid to die and that Jesus was waiting for him.

The nurse asked me to leave since it was horrible to see what Popsie was going through, and I told the nurse, "All my life I wanted to be a nurse and it didn't happen. I can be a nurse now in his last hours." For five hours, I stood at Popsie's side and held the tray for him while my brother Gary and my daughter Marsha emptied the tray, gave me clean trays, and provided a warm washcloth to wipe his face as they placed ice packs on his forehead. Once in a while, a tear would drop off my cheek and fall into the tray.

During his last hour, two of Popsie's brothers and all the siblings were in his room, me still by his side, stroking my fingers through his hair. At 1:30 p.m., he went to be with the Lord.

We had the funeral service the following Thursday. I continued staying at the trailer with Mom. The day after the funeral, I was sitting in the living room with Mom and some visiting friends. I suddenly felt very strange. I went outside where Rich was raking leaves and told him I had to get to ER. Once in ER, it didn't take long for them to tell me my blood pressure was extremely high. They wanted to admit me to the hospital, but I refused. The doctor wanted to know what had been going on the past few days, and I filled him in on what transpired for almost two weeks with my dad. His next question was, "Have you been able to cry?"

I replied, "No."

He said, "You have got to cry and let it all out to get better."

I told him we would go back to Grayling the next day and I would see my doctor.

After we got back to Mom's, I told Rich I had to have some time by myself. I drove to the fishing site. It was a cold day, and the clouds were very dark and ominous. It looked like it could storm anytime. I walked along the shoreline and told my Dad everything I didn't get to tell him when he was still alive. I cried so hard I was tired. I returned to the pickup and sat there just looking out over the lake and the stormy sky. While sitting there, I said, "Please, Lord, send me a sign that Popsie heard me." A minute or two later, the ugly, dark, ominous clouds parted over the middle of the lake. The center was a beautiful shade of blue, and suddenly there was a white cloud in the shape of an angel. Thank you, Lord; I know Popsie heard me.

The next day, we went back to Grayling. I went right to the doctor's office, where I was told I needed an appointment to see the doctor. I went past the receptionist and into the clinic hallway. (That was before they started locking doors.) I just said to the nurse, "Help me." She whisked me into a room and took my blood pressure, and before I knew it, the doctor was there beside me. I was sent home with medication and prescribed bed rest. I slept the next twenty-four hours with Rich checking on me to see that I was all right. Sunday was spent much the same. The doctor gave me permission to go back to the UP, and we were at Moms' again.

My sister-in-law, Sandy, spent the next month with Mom. Christmas Eve 1998, we started north to be with Mom over Christmas. We were caught in a whiteout near Gaylord and ended up in a ditch on the truck's right side. We had purchased the truck a week before and it only had 165 miles on it. There was lots of damage on the right side and we needed a new tire. Hours later, we were on the road again heading north, but by the time we arrived, it was too late to go to church services.

Mom decided she needed space and wanted to be by herself for a while. My uncle lived a mile down the road and would call her or come over every morning. Looking back on it now, she was such a courageous woman. She couldn't have done it without her faith in God. Her cough was really bad and she had to move slowly to do anything. Once, she was so hungry for a custard pie, she baked one. It took her hours. Every Sunday, she would dress up as she did when she was able to go to church, jewelry and all, and would listen to sermons on TV. She would read the Sunday paper that my uncle brought over and fix a nice meal for herself.

As long as I could remember, even from the years in Detroit, Mom always wore a hat to church. She had beautiful hats. She was an elegant dresser. When she passed away, sister-in-law Karen and I divided up her hats. When Rich and I moved to Engadine, I wore a hat to church. A short time later, Rich and I started attending church services in Newberry. I still wore Mom's hats. I was an usher for a while and not knowing many people there, I became known as "the hat lady." Years later, I met one woman in particular in Timber Charlie's restaurant who came up to me and said, "Aren't you the hat lady?"

Four months after Popsie's passing, we were home, and I was complaining about not finding a job. Mom said, "Maybe God has other plans for you. Maybe he wants you to stay with me till my end." We went home. I packed a suitcase and headed north. Rich would drive up on weekends. About two weeks later, my brother Gary, flew home and we talked about our childhood. Mom was so tired. One night, we told her that if she was holding on for us kids, she didn't have to. We would be fine. That was all she was waiting to hear, I am sure.

When we went to bed that night, she told me her funeral arrangements were made and then named who she wanted for pall-bearers. She had a beautiful red dress that she never wore and said my dad never got to see her in it. I said, "How about being buried in it? Then Popsie will get to see you wearing it." She agreed. She had removed her oxygen during the night thinking that by morning she would be gone, but it doesn't happen that fast. She stayed in bed the rest of her remaining time.

We called her pastor, who visited Mom almost every day. Each time she had requested her favorite passage, the twenty-third Psalm, "The Lord is my shepherd." Karen was a real nurse to Mom, bathing her and nursing her like a professional. Mom's last full day was a very good one. Her sister Angeline and brother Hank came over to the house, and they laughed, reminisced, and had a really good time. Allan recalls asking her what she wanted to eat, and she said strawberry shortcake. She ate it all!

For five days we all took care of her, and I barely left her side. I slept on the edge of the bed, sometimes under the covers with her, sometimes on top. I was exhausted by the fifth night. Late afternoon on the fifth day, my mother ordered me to sleep in another room so I could get some "real sleep." Her exact words to me were "If you don't get some sleep, you are going to beat me to the undertaker."

Don and Linda, Allan and Karen, Gary and Sandy were all home, and the women did the cooking and other caretaking chores. I skipped dinner, too tired to eat. I went to bed and slept until 6:00 a.m. Allan and Karen spent Mom's last night sleeping on either side of her. Her body was shutting down fast and they had her propped in a sitting position to breathe easier. A little after 6:00 a.m., I went into her room and saw it was just a matter of time now.

I stood by the bed and said, "Mom, I really had a good sleep. I am going to put the coffee on and sit with you. I hope you know how much I love you." I kissed her on the forehead, and she tried so hard to open her eyes but couldn't. She was able to nod her head yes, and

53

I knew she heard me. We were all in the bedroom with Mom, and at 8:42 a.m., after five months of struggling, she took her final breath.

Her wake was on Good Friday, and her funeral Saturday morning. As in the previous sixty-three years, my parents would once again be spending Easter together…this time with our Lord.

Chapter 4

We went back to Grayling, and I continued the volunteer work at the hospital for a couple more months. The following year, a dear friend of mine, Ernie McKeever, then living in South Carolina, was recovering from cancer surgery. I hadn't seen her in years. She had been taking care of her husband while living in Colorado, and he had recently passed after a long illness. Like my dad, she neglected to take care of herself while being a caregiver and she ended up with cancer. We drove to South Carolina and spent two days there. Ernie lived in assisted living. We visited her in July, and early December of that year she passed away.

In 2001, Rich and I made a trip out east. We visited most of the historical sites in Pennsylvania. We went on a tour and were paired up with a couple from Alabama. They were raised on farms as we had been, so we had a lot in common. They talked about cotton and pea-nut farming; we could share dairy and other crops like soybeans with them. We also spent time at the boardwalk before returning home.

In 2002, I received a phone call from cousin Eunice saying her husband had cancer. We talked on the phone every day. One morn-ing in March 2003, Eunice asked if I could come and spend about a week with her. Herb was nearing the end of his life, and she didn't want to be there alone. Her kids would be there later. I packed some clothes and left for Newberry. In the meantime, Rich and I had dis-cussed possibly moving to Engadine. Daughter Marsha, John, and family were living in Gould City, and it didn't make much sense to be in Grayling, with a two-and-a-half-hour trip to see the kids. I also had been doctoring with my right knee, which was giving me a lot of pain.

I spent a week with Eunice, and we discussed our possible move back to the UP. She told me Lorraine Leville was thinking about moving to Manistique to be near her daughter. Lorraine had been widowed a few years earlier. I drove out to Lorraine's house and asked her about selling it. I liked what I saw. She wanted to meet with her kids to establish a price.

Eunice's kids came home, and I went back to Grayling. I told Rich about the house for sale on M117. A few days later, we got the call that Herb had passed away peacefully. We came north for the funeral. During that time, we went to Lorraine's house so Rich could see it. She told us her asking price, and we said we would take it. She moved during the summer, and we moved in over Labor Day weekend.

About that time, my Uncle Hank was diagnosed with esophageal cancer. He had surgery and was very limited on what he could eat. Daughter Judy was with him for a while, and then he moved downstate to live with her.

I was doctoring in Petoskey with my right knee and was told I needed total knee replacement. We were barely settled in our new home when I had right knee replacement surgery in October 2003. The knee was not healing the way it should. I had constant pain and continued walking with a cane long after the surgery. Each time I would go back to the doctor, I didn't get much satisfaction. I had the knee drained twice of a weird-colored fluid with floating particles in it.

After a year of runaround, I got a second opinion from a doctor in Gaylord. He said he thought he could help me. I had surgery the following February. I found out I had the wrong prosthesis put in, and when the new doctor did the surgery, he had to get a much larger prosthesis because of all the additional damaged bone that had to be removed. He said, "You had a kneecap full of sawdust. I did the best I could with what I had left to work with." I also have permanent nerve damage in that knee. Recovery from that surgery went well.

Because I favored the right knee for so long, the left knee needed replacing. The same doctor did the surgery for the left knee six months later. It healed nicely with no problem. Because I still compensate for the right knee, the calf of the left leg is over two inches larger than the right.

With me being laid up for so long with both knees, Rich and I didn't get to travel anymore. A few months later, Rich was sent to a specialist in Marquette by our primary doctor because of problems he was having. Rich's kidneys were shutting down from all the years of drinking. He was told it wouldn't be long and that he would be on dialysis. That didn't stop the drinking. I would not drink with him, but that didn't slow him down.

Thanksgiving week 2005, we were at the hospital in Marquette where Rich had a port put in for dialysis. The weather was horrid with a snowstorm, and we had to spend Thanksgiving Day in the hospital. Saturday, we went home, and the following Monday, he started his dialysis treatments in Newberry, sitting in a chair for three hours, eighteen minutes, three times a week. In February, the water in Newberry was declared contaminated and unsuitable for dialysis; all the patients were sent to Marquette for treatment. We lived in the hospitality rooms at the hospital. We were able to fix meals in the kitchen of that area. It was our home away from home. All we could do was read and watch TV. I cross-stitched a baby quilt while there. We would leave for Marquette on Monday morning and return home on Saturday morning. This went on from February until Memorial Day weekend 2006.

Starting in June, we were back in Newberry with dialysis. Rich's body was really slowing down. He was very tired most days and he knew his time was getting short. He would make remarks to me like "You will have a lot of beautiful memories of trips we have taken." We had a garage sale, and he was too tired to help me with it. There were also days I didn't want to be around him because of his resentful attitude about being on dialysis. Life was not so pleasant since he would not give up drinking, and I resented it very much. I was also sorry for what drinking I did do with him through our early years of marriage, but it was too late; the damage had been done.

On Sunday morning, July 16, 2006, we went to church and had communion; the day was great. I had made our favorite meal, which consisted of mashed potatoes and gravy, pork roast, and cucumbers and cream. We spent the afternoon playing our favorite card game Malice and Spite. In the evening, we watched movies. It was the best day we had had in a long time. There was a lot of reminiscing over places we had traveled and people we had become good friends with from lots of states.

I was still sleeping in the La-Z-Boy because of my knees, and my back was not that great. Every night before Rich would go to bed, he would walk to the kitchen, get a drink of water, kiss me good-night, and go to bed. That Sunday night, he went to the kitchen, got his drink of water, and walked to the dining room table area. He leaned on a chair and said, "No matter what happens, just know how much I love you." He kissed me goodnight and went to bed.

Around 2:30 a.m., he called to me to get the floor fan and turn it on in the bedroom. Within a half hour later, he was out of bed and sweating. I got him sitting on a chair in the dining room, grabbed the phone, called 911, and told them my husband was having a heart attack. (The specialist had told me months before that he would die of a heart attack.) I called my cousin, who called our pastor and his wife, and they arrived at the hospital shortly after the ambulance arrived. Time was running out fast, and we were all at Rich's side with the pastor reciting the twenty-third Psalm. Within forty-five minutes after arriving at the hospital, he went to be with the Lord. It was exactly seven months to the day of when he went on dialysis July 17, 2006. He was seventy-four years old. I was sixty-eight.

During the next two months, I had more garage sales and sold all of Rich's guns, fishing equipment, fishing sinkers, and the molds to make the sinkers. While Mark was home for the funeral, I had him pick out any tools he would like to have. I told the kids I would be out west in fall to deliver them.

September 29, 2006, I struck out for Colorado Springs. It was the first time I ever drove that far by myself, but I felt very confident since Rich and I had made the trips so many times in the past. The first night I spent in Illinois, I bought some fast food and headed for a motel. The second night was spent in Hays, Kansas, and I felt very awkward going into a restaurant by myself. I hadn't done that in years. Halfway through my meal, a couple sitting near me started a conversation, and I was all right after that. I listened to music as I drove, and it seemed like miles of sunflower fields on both sides of the highway. I was thinking about all the trips we had made together across country.

Suddenly, I had the strangest thing happen. I guess I could describe it as a vision. Rich was behind the wheel, I was in the passenger seat, and as he often did when driving, he leaned over the steering wheel and, looking directly at me, said, "I love you, darling." He had a big smile on his face. Just like that, I was back behind the wheel driving and wondering, *What just happened?*

I spent two weeks with Mark, Eva, and Eric. I had taken Rich's saw to Mark along with a couple of other tools. Mark often remarked that it was the best saw he ever used and would say, "Thanks, Rich." I then drove to Albuquerque and spent two weeks with Kathy, Scott, Chris, and Jordan. The days flew by, and I was on my way home.

I was fine until I reached the Texas border, and there stood this huge sign saying "Welcome to Texas." The state where Rich and I began our life together. Then the tears started. I stopped in Groom, TX, where we had stopped before. At the time, I wanted to see what was added to where the huge cross stood; you could see it for miles. I walked the Stations of the Cross, visited the tomb, and saw the table for the Lord's Supper. At that time, only two bronze people were sitting at the table. I am sure it has been completed by now.

I was sitting on a bench talking with a lady from California who was taking pictures. I said, "I sure wish my husband could have seen this."

And she replied, "What makes you think he isn't seeing it?"

I proceeded on my way and cried all the way to Oklahoma City. Once I was out of Oklahoma, I pulled myself up by my bootstraps and said out aloud, "Okay, girl, you are about to start a new life." I arrived home early November. The first holidays without your mate are not easy, but you get through it, and every year after that it gets easier.

Every morning, I continued listening/watching Joyce Meyer, John Hagee, and Joel Osteen. I also did a lot of reading. I continued attending church in Newberry. Eunice and I spent a lot of time together growing up, and both of us being widowed, we talked almost every day. I still loved working on my crafts and attending craft shows.

In October of 2007, Eunice and I went to St. Louis, where she watched a grandson play high school football. Soon we were on our way to Virginia, where we were going to spend a few days with Janet Yeske. I had not seen her since I graduated in 1955. That year the drought was really bad in the south, and we were amazed at the huge cracks in the farmland ground in Tennessee. The drive was beautiful going through the Shenandoah Valley with all the trees at their peak colors. We drove on the Blue Ridge Parkway, which was a challenge with all the curves and narrow roads. We were glad to finally get on the main highway to get us to Janet's.

What a reunion the three of us had for the next five days. We would be up early in the morning, drinking coffee and talking, and it continued until late at night. We did attend a huge craft show one day, and one afternoon we drove to a casino in West Virginia. It was hard to leave because we knew we would never all be together ever again. Janet had a lot of health issues and ended up on dialysis. She passed away in April 2013.

On our way home, we stopped at Gettysburg and took a bus tour of the town and battlefield. We also stopped at the Hershey Factory in Hershey, PA. For Christmas 2010, Mark, Marsha, and Kathy, along with their spouses, gave me a round-trip ticket to Albuquerque and Colorado Springs. I wanted to get away from all the snow. I had been fighting bronchitis since October and couldn't seem to shake it. I flew west in early January. I had a horrid cough, which I took with me to Albuquerque. Every day that I was there, I seemed to feel a little better. Every day I would go for a long walk with their dog, Kalli. I enjoyed seeing all the southwest homes again; it brought back a lot of good memories of my years in San Antonio. The warmer weather sure felt good.

While Jordan was in school and Kathy and Scott were at work, I was busy reading books. I also cross-stitched a baby quilt Kathy didn't get around to working on. It was a much-needed vacation.

Every morning, I would be up around 6:00 a.m., make a cup of coffee, and read. One morning, I asked Jordan to turn on the TV before she left for school. (There were so many remotes to operate that I hadn't learned yet.) I was surfing the channels when I came across Joyce Meyer. It was a Monday morning, and that week she was speaking about the Fruits of the Spirit. I watched her every morning; it was so uplifting. I ordered the series to be sent home to Michigan. Between reading my inspirational books and listening to Joyce every morning, I knew I would be going home a new person, more relaxed and closer to God than ever before.

The month of January flew by, and I was on my way to Colorado Springs, to be with Mark, Eva, and Eric for the month of February. By the time I got there, my cough was gone, and I felt better than I had in months. The weather was nice; they didn't get much snow, and what they did get melted fast. The kids had a park behind their house, so every morning I would be out walking. I really enjoyed my time in Colorado Springs, and before I knew it, it was March 2 and time for me to fly home.

I had purchased Joyce Meyer's book *The Confident Woman*, which I intended to read on my flight back to Michigan. Mark drove me to the airport in Denver only to find that all flights where running late due to a seven-inch snowfall in Atlanta the night before. In the meantime, the airline attendant couldn't find me scheduled for any flight. It took another half hour for her to find the reservation. During that time, Mark and I just stood there and talked. Because of the long wait, I was not charged for my overweight luggage. The attendant thanked me for being so patient and not giving her a hard time. I informed her that I had a daughter working for Southwest Airlines and I was very much aware of what she had to put up with concerning irate people.

My flight was delayed forty-five minutes, and I was on my way to the Minneapolis airport, where I was to change planes for Detroit. The weather was nice, and the flight was good. Once in Minneapolis, I was told there would be another delay for my flight to Detroit. I was given my boarding pass and was at the end of a very long line. What happened next was a conversation I will never forget.

While standing in line, an elderly gentleman struck up a conversation with me. He was traveling to Fort Lauderdale with his grandson after spending three weeks in Germany. He asked me where I was from, and I replied, "The Upper Peninsula of Michigan." I then had to explain just where that was located. He asked me where I had been and for how long. I proceeded to tell him I had spent the month of January with a daughter and family I hadn't seen in two and a half years before going on to Colorado Springs to spend the month with my son and family whom I had not seen in over three years. He commented on how good it would feel to be back home again after being gone for a while, and I agreed that it's nice to be gone but there is no place like home.

We stood in line for a long time, and finally the line moved slowly ahead. I never saw so many people with carry-on luggage as I did that day. The elderly gentleman and grandson were just ahead of me. I would guess it was close to ten minutes from when we talked to when we were near the entrance door of the plane. Finally the gentleman stepped into the plane, the flight attendant saying, "Welcome aboard flight—" Before I knew it, he had backed out of the plane, turned, stood in front of me, and said, "You look like you are at such peace."

I replied, "I am."

He said, "I know it. It is written all over you." He then turned to enter the plane.

My seat was near the front of the plane, and I didn't see him nearby. I assumed he was seated further back in the plane. All during the flight from Minneapolis to Detroit, I thought, *What a strange thing for this man to say to me.*

We arrived in Detroit late, and I was waiting for my wheelchair and attendant to take me to the gate for my flight to Marquette. I knew there was no way I could get to the gate on time without a fast runner. While standing there, I suddenly felt a hand on my left shoulder. It was this elderly gentleman I had talked with earlier. He was about an arm's length away. Walking very slowly, not stopping, and looking straight ahead, he said to me, "May you have a long and happy life."

I replied, "Thank you, I wish you the same."

I watched him walk about another fifteen feet forward, and all of a sudden, he was gone! I will never forget my time spent with my airport angel.

About that time, an attendant was there with a wheelchair for me. He just said, "Hang on," and his two legs just flew through the airport to get me to the next gate. Just as he got me to the ticket counter, my flight pulled out for Marquette. Another couple from Marquette had missed their flight. We were told we would be put up at a hotel for the night and could catch a 10:00 a.m. flight to Marquette in the morning.

I immediately called Marsha. I knew John was in route to Marquette (an hour and a half's drive) to pick me up, and I had to stop him. Her first question was "Are you all right?" to which I answered, "I have never been better." Thank goodness for cell phones. She was able to stop him before he got too many miles down the road.

We were put up in a hotel and given vouchers for food. I was to meet the couple in the lounge as soon as I was settled in my room. I called Kathy, and her first question was, "Are you all right?" to which I answered, "I have never been better."

The final call was to Mark. His first question was, "Are you all right?" and again I answered, "I have never been better." I then proceeded to the lounge. I introduced myself to the couple from Marquette only to find out she was the daughter of a schoolteacher in Engadine, and her sister graduated with my daughter. Another couple who had missed their flight to Windsor, Ontario, sat with us; they were just returning from a cruise. We must have sat in the lounge three hours talking. Somehow the subject turned to angels and whether we believed in them. We also shared our faith in God.

When I went to bed that night, I thanked God for the safe flight, my encounter with my airport angel, and the new friends I had met that night. The next morning, my new friends and I were able to catch our flight to Marquette with no delays. The flight home from out west was the start of a wonderful 2010 for me.

I was home less than a month when my cousin Eunice and I drove to Grand Rapids, where we went to a two-and-a-half-day conference by Joyce Meyer. It was great, and once again we met a lot of people. It was so nice to see Joyce in person after seeing her so many times on TV. We spent the last of the third day doing a little shopping and then headed for home. A short time later, my granddaughter Leah graduated from high school.

I had had my VFW Auxiliary membership transferred to Engadine, and once my knees were healed, I started attending the meetings. Only a few women attended. A short time after Rich died, I volunteered to cut cakes for the VFW fish fries. Betty Matchinske, who was a relative through marriage, offered to work with me; we became very good friends. She used to live in Chicago, and I was out west for eighteen years, so we had never had a chance to really visit. We had numerous fish fries during the summer. Betty was about twenty years older than me and had been widowed for a while. I would take her to doctor appointments, and we would shop and just visit, enjoying each other's company.

My uncle Richard died in 2004, and until that time I had not seen much of him or my Aunt Elsie, who also happened to be my godmother. When we were at the cemetery for my uncle's burial, Aunt Elsie asked me to visit her more, and I promised I would. Between healing from two knee surgeries, and Rich going on dialysis, I didn't get to keep that promise until 2006. Aunt Elsie attended Rich's funeral along with her son, Ron, and wife, Charlene. It was soon after that that I would call her or drive over to visit her. She lived about three miles from me. Often, I would call and tell her not to make anything for supper, that I would be bringing food over. I always made enough that she had leftovers.

She loved blackberry brandy. She drank it from a little glass in the shape of a boot. When I visited, we usually sat at the kitchen table. I wouldn't have been there long before she would say, "Shirley, is it too early?" or "Shirley, it's time," depending on the time of day. She would point toward the cupboard where the brandy was in, and I would promptly go get our glasses and pour us a shot of blackberry brandy.

Early 2010, Betty and I attended a church dinner at Bethlehem Lutheran. It was at that dinner that I was introduced to Lloyd Smith. He was a widower who had moved from Holly, Michigan, to Gould City in 2004. Marsha and John had known him for several years as Lloyd had dug a trench for their wood-burner setup. We would see each other once a month when we attended the church dinners.

One day Betty, and I attended a senior citizens dinner at the township hall in Engadine. We were standing in line to get our food, and I happened to be standing behind Lloyd. He was telling the person in front of him that he sold his Equinox to a guy down the road who needed a car for his daughter who was going to start college. I asked him if he sold it to John Blanchard. He said yes, and I said, "He is my son-in-law, and the daughter is my granddaughter." Before then, whenever I asked John who he had bought the car from, he would just say, "A nice man down the road."

Shortly after that, Betty needed back surgery in Marquette. I took her up there and stayed there until she was ready to come home. I brought her home on a Wednesday afternoon; the church dinner was that night. I put her to bed and went to the supper. I was going to bring her a carry-out dinner. There were about ten of us sitting at this big table, and in conversation I mentioned that I would have to teach Betty an easier way to hook up her seat belt so she wouldn't have to twist so much. Lloyd was sitting about three chairs from me and he said, "She needs a seat belt clip." I had never heard of them.

After dinner, I picked up Betty's dinner. Lloyd said he would show me the seat belt clip he had in his car. We ended up talking about many things in the parking lot for about thirty minutes until it started to rain. He said he had more clips at home and would give me some for Betty and myself. I took Betty her dinner, spent the night, and stayed until her son got there the next day from Tennessee. Betty healed from her surgery quickly.

About two weeks after the conversation with Lloyd in the church parking lot, I attended a fish fry dinner in Naubinway. Lloyd and I sat together. When we were ready to go home, he said he had seat belt clips for Betty and me. He proceeded to put mine on in my car. I then told him about a problem I was having with my car, and him being the mechanic he was, he said he would take a look at it if I came over to his place.

I took the car over to his house about three days later, and it didn't take him long to find the problem. It was a cold April day. We ended up sitting in the car and talking a long time when I told him I was going to have to leave because I was getting very cold. He asked me into the house and said he had something to show me in the garage. He uncovered a beautiful white 1960 Chevy Impala trimmed in blue. It was gorgeous. I was very familiar with that year of car since I had graduated in 1955. (When I lived in Lansing after graduation, I owned a 1957 Ford Fairlane.) I went into the house to warm up, and we talked again for three hours or more. He told me about his life, and I told him about mine. He asked me out to dinner that night and that was the start of a beautiful friendship. I still say the seat belt clips brought us together.

Lloyd had a beautiful black Lab/German shepherd named Samantha. She went everywhere with him. He'd had her since she was a pup. They were attached at the hip. Other than to the neighbors next door, Lloyd didn't go anywhere except when he did work for other people. He was also on the Gould City Volunteer Fire Dept. In his nine years there, he didn't attend many functions either. He kept to himself with Samantha. I invited him to different functions, especially at school, since I had two grandkids in school in Engadine. In July, he took me downstate to meet his three sons.

In June of 2011, my daughter Marsha and I flew standby to Albuquerque for my granddaughter Jordan's high school graduation. What a trip. It was about the same time colleges were having their graduations, and we kept getting "bumped" in Chicago. We finally made it to Phoenix, where we slept on a bench at the airport. We had been in airports a total of fourteen hours. We arrived in Phoenix at midnight and got the first flight out for Albuquerque. Never again.

A lot of family members were there for the graduation, and one day we took a train to Santa Fe touring the churches. One highlight was the Church of Loretto. When living in San Antonio, I had read about that church in *Guideposts*, never dreaming I would ever get to see it. So far, I have been to that church three times. While I was there in Albuquerque, I called Lloyd two or three times, telling him of the beauty of the Sandia Mountains and how when the sun set in the evening, the mountains looks like gold. Quite a change from Michigan.

Lloyd was really into antique cars and would go downstate every year to the Woodward Cruise. We also attended the St. Ignace car shows. One year, he had the '60 Impala entered. As time went on, I also became deeply interested in the antique cars. We entered his car in a car show in his hometown of Mayville, and he won a trophy for best of the show in that category. Late summer of 2011, Lloyd, Samantha, and I drove to Carlisle, Pennsylvania, and attended the Corvette show they have every year.

I put my house up for sale and moved to Gould City in August 2011. My grandson Andrew played both football and basketball, and we attended all the home and away games.

John's cousin held "extravaganzas" each summer where he had a Grand Ole Opry star perform in his backyard. It would draw quite a crowd. The first one we saw was Jimmy Fortune, formerly with the Statler Brothers. He was advertising a cruise he was sponsoring for January to February of 2012. We spent some time with Jimmy, and he told us where we would be going on the cruise. Lloyd had been on a couple of cruises in the past, but this was to be my first one. There were about six to seven couples that signed up for the cruise besides me and Lloyd. We left from New Orleans with three stops: Jamaica; Cayman Islands; and Cozumel, Mexico.

We returned to New Orleans around noon on Saturday the day before the Super Bowl was to be held there. Not a motel available for miles. We were planning on driving to Florida and spending a couple of days with my brother Allan and his wife, Karen, who were spending the winter there. We were almost out of city limits when smoke was coming from the left front wheel. It didn't take long for Lloyd to see that the brake caliber was the culprit. Just ahead of us was a small privately owned garage. What were the odds of having a garage so close to where we started curling smoke?

We limped to the shop, and by that time it was already 4:00 p.m. We were met at the door by a small, very polite Vietnamese man. Lloyd told him the problem. The man said he would be able to fix it for us but would have to send a "runner" to pick up the part in another city, and that wouldn't be in until morning. He would be glad to fix it for us but not until he returned from church! Thank you, Lord. Another case of divine intervention. Who would work on Sunday, especially when it was Super Bowl Sunday? We were able to drive the car slow and he sent us to a motel close by. They had one room left! Was that God or what?

The next morning after church, he was at the shop. It took a couple of hours to do the job, but by early afternoon, we were on our way to Florida. We will never forget what he did for us. When we thanked him profusely, his only comment was "If I were where you were yesterday, I would want someone to help me." We will never forget his kindness.

We arrived in Florida just as the game was to begin. We arrived just in time for the Super Bowl party. Lots of food and visiting. We spent a couple of days there before we left for Georgia. There we headed for Barbara's goat farm. I had known Barbara from living in San Antonio, as she worked at Audie Murphy Hospital in the office.

We spent about four days with Barbara and learned a lot about goats. All of her goats were show goats, so she did well at auctions where a lot of the buyers knew what good stock she had. One day we spent in Savannah, Georgia. What a city; so much of original buildings still in place.

We arrived home on Valentine's Day. There was a deep layer of snow and ice in the driveway after heavy snowfalls while we were gone plus a couple of rainfalls that left ice all over. What a cleanup. Lloyd then announced we would never be taking another trip anywhere in the winter!

Aunt Elsie's health was getting worse by the month. I would visit her and take her to the doctor when needed. On December 9, 2010, she turned a hundred years old. I baked a cake for her, and through the day, her son was there along with nieces and nephews. Ron had lost his wife to cancer a couple of years earlier. In November, Ron called me to say that Aunt Elsie had called him: something was going on. Lloyd and I immediately left for Aunt Elsie's house driving separate cars. It was obvious she needed to get to the hospital. She was able to walk so we put her in my car, and Lloyd called the hospital to let them know we were on our way. It was so much faster than waiting for an ambulance would have been. She was admitted to the hospital and spent the next two days there. She moved in with Ron in Manistique when she was discharged.

About a month into her stay with Ron, it was obvious she needed more care than Ron could give her. She was admitted to the Medicare part of the hospital. On December 9, 2011, Aunt Elsie's hundred-and-first birthday, Ron, Lloyd, and I, armed with a bottle of blackberry brandy, entered her room and we celebrated her birthday. It was a joyous occasion, especially since no one in the immediate family had lived to that age.

In March 2012, I got a call from Ron saying Aunt Elsie had taken a turn for the worse. I drove to Manistique so I could be with Ron and his son, Merle; Merle's wife, Marie; and their children. She put in a bad day, and we finally requested that all medication be decreased or stopped. Merle and family went home in the evening, and nurses brought in lounge chairs for me and Ron to sleep in through the night

In the morning, Ron went home to let his dog out and feed her. I stretched out in the lounge chair to get more sleep. I had just dozed off when all of a sudden, I heard nothing. I woke in a hurry and was by her side when she drew her last breath. I was glad she wasn't alone and that I was there since she was my godmother. She had lived a hundred and one years and three months. I felt bad that she didn't live a few weeks longer so she would have known about Lloyd's and my covenant commitment, which took place on April 14.

April 2012, Lloyd and I exchanged a covenant commitment at Naubinway Christian Fellowship Church. Lloyd's three sons were there, as were Marsha, John, and some friends. We had a beautiful reception at the Blanchard home. It was the start of a whole new life again for the both of us.

In June, we took a scenic route through secondary roads and drove to Colorado Springs where my grandson Eric graduated from high school. It was the last time our whole family was together. Eric went on to college and graduated from the Air Force Academy. Lloyd and I attended his graduation; it was the most impressive event we have ever attended.

On December 31, 2012, Lloyd had right knee replacement surgery. He was fine the first thirty-six hours. We walked down the hallway New Year's Day and expected to go home soon. Monday, they gave him Norco for pain. I stayed at the hospital, so I was in his room early in the morning. He decided to sit in a chair to eat breakfast, and a nurse helped him get situated. She turned to get his bedding ready. I was standing next to his bed. All of a sudden, Lloyd's eyes rolled back. He was unconscious.

I hollered to the nurse, and she told me to run for help. Two nurses got him into bed but couldn't get a pulse. He was unresponsive, and the next thing I knew we had a Code Blue. The room filled with people, a crash cart, and me backing up against the wall. I felt like I was watching a scene from a movie. Just as they were about to use the paddles, they were able to feel a pulse. They rushed him to ICU on another floor, where he remained the next twenty-four hours. In the course of twenty-four hours, he had five different specialists trying to find out what happened. Every time a therapist would get Lloyd up and walking, he took a few steps and would pass out. Other than getting him out of bed, he had no therapy on the knee.

After fourteen days, he was told he would have to go to the hospital in Newberry. Still no answers. After getting him settled, a therapist in Newberry had him up, trying to walk. He passed out again. The second day, I told the therapist I couldn't watch more of the same and I went home. We had been gone from home fourteen days, but once in Newberry, I was able to go home as it was only about 35 miles away.

Once home, I got in my La-Z-Boy, really needing a nap. Before drifting off, I prayed, "Lord, please give *somebody* the answer as to why Lloyd keeps passing out." I fell into a sound sleep, and at 8:00 p.m., a voice woke me up saying, "It's like your mother." I spent the next two hours trying to figure out what those words meant but I was only thinking of the past ten years of my mom's life.

I went to bed at 10:00 p.m., and once again prayed, "Lord, I know you are trying to give me an answer, but I'm not getting it." At 2:10 a.m., the same voice, the same four words, "It's like your mother," woke me up. Instantly, I had the answer. When Mom was in her fifties, she was in the hospital being treated for something she didn't have, and the drugs almost killed her. Lloyd was passing out because of the Norco given to him for pain.

I got on the computer and looked up the side effects of Norco. Seven were listed, and Lloyd had all seven. At 5:00 a.m., I was on my way to the hospital. The first thing I told Lloyd when I got there was not to take anything for pain until we talked with his doctor. When his doctor finished up in ER, he came to Lloyd's room. I showed him the seven side effects, and he agreed Lloyd had all seven. After a little hesitation, the doctor said, "I think you are right." He was taken off all pain medication.

Lloyd had been without something for pain a full twenty-four hours when he fell asleep that Saturday evening. Around midnight, he started sweating and didn't stop for hours. By morning, all the drugs were sweated out of him. I took him home on Monday.

We had been planning a driving trip to Alaska for months. All the arrangements were made, and we were to leave on the following Saturday morning. Lloyd had been feeling very tired and just not up to par. Doctors couldn't find anything wrong. On Monday morning, he really felt awful. He finally told me we would have to cancel the trip because he wouldn't be able to drive feeling the way he did. He had been doctoring but not really getting any answers. We finally said we needed answers. We arranged to see doctors at Mayo Clinic, and two days later we were on our way to Rochester, Minnesota. After four days of numerous tests and doctors, he was diagnosed with sleep apnea. His dentist made a special mouthpiece for him to wear and has had no problems with that since.

May 26, 2015, I had total right hip replacement. One and a half days later, I went home and started therapy. I have very high pain tolerance because of my allergies to pain medication. The more therapy I had, the worse the pain was. After ten days, I went back to the doctor to have the stitches out and get X-rayed. Besides replacing the hip, the doctor had fractured my hip and didn't know it. The bone had now separated. I had a choice: go back to surgery and have a pin put in or be in a wheelchair until new cartilage grew around it. I opted for the wheelchair.

I had to go back for X-rays every three weeks. I was in a wheelchair until September 19, 2015. During that time, I learned just how much you have to depend on someone else to do things for you. Having been very independent most of my life, it was hard for me to accept. I now help anyone I can who is confined to a wheelchair. Especially in a grocery store. How fortunate we are when we have two legs to walk with.

I was still working on crafts and decided craft shows weren't fun anymore without someone to be with me like in the past. What really made me decide to hang it up was the last show I was in; I had a monk's cloth afghan stolen. I then started cross-stitching a king-size quilt. It took me three years to complete. My daughter Marsha is the owner of it. Since then, I have made a cross-stitched quilt for my daughter Kathy. That one took me a little over two years to make.

Leah graduated from college, and Andrew was playing high school football and basketball. Lloyd and I attended every game we could, both home and away.

In 2014, Lloyd started having pain in his left side. After several MRI's and ultrasounds, he was diagnosed with a cyst on the left kidney. A specialist drained it, but the pain persisted. He has had injections in his spine, nerves burned on both sides of lower back, and still the pain remains.

In June 2014, we purchased a travel trailer. We had hopes of using it a lot, but it didn't happen. We did drive up to the Ft. Wilkinson campground in the Copper Country of the Upper Peninsula. We drove to the campground over Labor Day and spent a week there. What beauty. It was so quiet. We spent a lot of time outside. The weather was beautiful. It was there I read *Welcome, Holy Spirit* and *Lord, I Need a Miracle* by Benny Hinn. I never felt closer to God than I did during our five days in the campground.

In 2015, Lloyd purchased a '52, two-door Bellaire hardtop that was to be his dream car. He needed to rebuild the whole thing. Lloyd and his son Alan drove to Memphis, Tennessee, and bought a 2011 Camaro motor V6 with a six-speed automatic transmission. The car was gutted, and so began the long process of putting it together. He was able to work on the frame and floor of the car, and then had to quit because he needed left knee replacement surgery.

Once again, we went through the same scenario as the first. The same doctor, different pain medication, different hospital. Brought Lloyd home from the hospital, took little to no pain medication. The first morning home while walking, he had to sit down. He passed out. ER said he was just dehydrated. The next morning, the same thing happened. I had to call 911. He was unconscious a half hour before the ambulance arrived. He ended up in a hospital downstate, and after three days, they found out it was the Percocet he took for pain which was very minimal. Once he sweated it out, I was able to bring him home. The only thing he takes for pain since is Tylenol, regardless of how much pain he has.

We didn't get to do much camping after that. We worked on projects around the property and put in a new front lawn. We did a lot of trimming on the beautiful pine trees behind the house. There were always a ton of leaves to rake up from the maples in the front yard.

The kids gave me a birthday party when I turned eighty. It was one of the biggest highlights of my life. My church family was there, along with many friends and relatives. My Uncle Ervin was there, which I really enjoyed; he was in his late nineties and couldn't get around very well anymore. He was also my favorite of all uncles. My eightieth birthday is one of the most memorable of my life.

Chapter

5

In 2014, my brother Allan was having lung issues. A pulmonary specialist, Dr. Sabbaq, diagnosed him with familial idiopathic pulmonary fibrosis. It is hereditary; my Mom had died from it at age eighty. Just two years later, I was having breathing problems. After ending up in ER on one occasion, it was obvious I needed to see my brother's doctor. I had my first appointment in November 2016. I was scheduled for a lung biopsy on December 22.

The Sunday before we went downstate, I received a gift at church from Dale and Yvonne St. Andre. That gift changed my life in many ways. I received a devotional, *Jesus Calling*, and a journal. Up until then, I did a lot of reading, mainly books by pastors, but I was not one to spend time with God every day in reading the Bible or praying. I made a promise to God that once I returned home after the biopsy, I would have time set aside for *him* every day. I have kept that promise. I am so thankful for the gift from Dale and Yvonne. It really changed my life.

Lloyd's birthday was December 21. He turned seventy-five. I had hoped to have a small party for him for that milestone, but instead we drove to Pontiac, and his big treat was having dinner at Cracker Barrel. Not what I had planned, but he never complained.

I had the lung biopsy on December 22 in Rochester Hills. It showed I did indeed have familial idiopathic pulmonary fibrosis. We stayed with Lloyd's son Gordon, and his other sons Alan and Darrin came over to Gordon's for Christmas dinner. We had to wait seventy-two hours before we could leave for home in case I had to go back to the hospital.

I loved going to bingo and had been doing so for many years in Gould City. I didn't win much, but it was a nice night out and I got to visit with a lot of people I knew. One of my best friends was Miz Salter. I knew Miz for at least sixty years plus. She is one of several people who did not condemn me for leaving Larry. During the years in San Antonio and Colorado Springs, plus the six years in Grayling, Miz always wrote to me. We corresponded with each other over my eighteen years away from Engadine.

Miz's daughter, Jackie, graduated from high school with my daughter Marsha. Jackie spent time on our dairy farm in their childhood years, especially during the summer. Jackie was in the Air Force, and I always knew where she was stationed from Miz's letters. Jackie had retired from the Air Force and was living in Arizona.

I managed to go to most of Andrew's basketball games that winter, and Lloyd attended all of the games. The cold didn't help my breathing, and I had to wear a mask when outside. I was becoming more limited on how much I could do in a day.

During the summer months of 2017, I was able to still plant flowers in my flowerbeds and do minimal things outside with Lloyd. We took in Andrew's football games both at home and away. Once basketball season started, I knew I wouldn't be able to attend all the basketball games, but I did get to see some. Andrew was a very good player, and I missed not being able to cheer him on. When the basketball season ended in his senior year, we were thrilled to find out that Andrew had broken five school records for basketball and two for football. We are so proud of him. He is now attending Alma College in Michigan.

Lloyd was still going prairie dog hunting every April, with his sons in Lubbock, Texas. I had put in a really rough winter with my breathing and at times couldn't talk above a whisper. I missed being able to sing at church and go places. I was missing more and more of Andrew's basketball games. Some days, I would be too tired to cook or to wash dishes. One weekend, I slept twenty-one of twenty-four hours. Shortly after that, I was in bed, extremely tired. Breathing was not good, and I could literally feel the life going out of my body. I found myself saying, "Lord, help me," and I was soon breathing better. When Lloyd came home from prairie dog hunting, I told him I could not spend another winter in Gould City or I would be dead.

I wanted to spend a winter in Arizona to see if my breathing would improve. We had the travel trailer, but I wanted something bigger (against Lloyd's wishes). I bought a 2007, thirty-four-foot Montana fifth wheel. After surfing the Internet, I found an RV park in Tucson. We waited until after Thanksgiving to leave for Arizona so Lloyd's three sons could spend Thanksgiving with us (which they did for many years). It was the first trip for both of us to Arizona. I named it "our trip from hell." Anything that could go wrong did on our trip. There were motor problems, and a windstorm where we drove miles and got five mpg. Then a four-hour delay sitting on a major highway in Texas because of a fire, and a whiteout snowstorm in New Mexico. We finally arrived at the RV Park two days late.

We started walking every morning. To circle the park took exactly one mile, and within three weeks we were walking a mile in twenty-two minutes! I felt great. My breathing was better, and I could do things I hadn't done in a long time. We met a lot of nice people in the park (mostly snowbirds), and I attended a Bible Study held in the clubhouse every Wednesday. We also attended church services in the clubhouse every Sunday. My brother Allan and Karen have a place in a park in Apache Junction, so we visited them while we were here.

My dear friend Chris Walker, who lives in San Antonio, has her daughter Janet and son Ricky living with her. When we were about two days into our drive to Tucson, I received a call from Janet saying Chris had had a bad stroke. She was unable to talk and there was not much movement on her right side. We kept in touch by phone, and in January, Janet called, and I heard Chris say, "Hi, Shirleeee." It was wonderful.

Through the years, Chris and I talked about seeing each other "one more time," but for one reason or another, mostly sickness, we were unable to get together. Until her stroke, we talked to each other once a week on the phone. I asked Lloyd if we could drive to San

Antonio so Chris and I could see each other one more time. Without hesitation, he said, "When do we go?" Chris seemed to improve a little each week, and after talking to Janet, we told her we would come down Valentine's Day weekend. It was a twelve-hundred-mile trip.

I had not been to San Antonio in forty-four years, so needless to say, nothing looked the same. We stayed at a fabulous hotel alongside Cornerstone Church. We drove to the rehab place that Chris was in on Valentine's Day and had a wonderful visit. After forty-four years of wishing, we were together again. She couldn't talk much but still had the hearty laugh that I grew to love. The next morning, we attended church services at Cornerstone; it was wonderful to hear John Hagee preach again. We met with Matthew after the service. That afternoon, we visited Chris again, and in the evening attended church services where they held a "Cowboy night," which was a BBQ in one of the buildings. We met a lot of people again. Monday morning, we struck out for home.

Jackie and Al had moved from Arizona to Gould City in November 2014. Jackie's dad had passed away, and Miz was not in good health. They bought a home in Curtis. Jackie was at bingo every week with Miz, so during that time we became very close. Miz became very sick and was in several hospitals but didn't get any answers. Jackie and her brother, Dennis, drove her to Mayo Clinic in Rochester, Minnesota. She was admitted to the hospital and was diagnosed with SIBO (small intestinal bacterial overgrowth). Miz came home from the hospital and was on hospice for five and a half weeks.

Miz passed away in August 2017. Al spent most of his life in Arizona, so the move to Michigan was quite a sacrifice on his part. Jackie's rheumatoid arthritis hit with a vengeance that winter. By spring, they both knew they wanted to go back to Arizona. They put the house up for sale; it sold in three days. After Memorial Day, they were on their way back to Arizona. They purchased a beautiful home in Green Valley.

Lloyd and I saw a lot of Jackie and Al our first winter here, and we spent both Christmas and New Year's with them. Jackie would go to bingo with me at the clubhouse on Thursday nights, and Al would be watching movies with Lloyd in our fifth wheel. The longer we were here, the more we knew this would be where we would spend our winters. During the winter, Lloyd and I checked out many campgrounds both in Tucson and Apache Junction. We had made a deposit on our "space" for the next winter. One day, Allan and Karen drove down from Apache Junction and spent the day with us in our fifth wheel. We invited Al and Jackie over as well since Jackie is a first cousin to Karen and they hadn't seen each other in a while. We all had a good visit.

One morning, while out for our mile walk, I asked Lloyd if he could live in the park nine or ten months of the year. He said he could but would then want to get rid of the property in Gould City so he wouldn't be paying taxes on something we were not living in. About two hours later, we walked to the clubhouse to pick up our mail. There on the bulletin board was a mobile home for sale. It had been posted the night before. Once again…divine intervention.

We called the sellers and asked if we could look at their home. It was on a double lot. I fell in love with it. We were just two weeks from having to go back to Michigan. Everything moved very fast, and on March 18, 2019, I became owner of the home. It was completely furnished, but we knew we would want our own things in it. Lloyd also wanted a shed put on the property so he could work on woodcrafts and other things. Before we left for Michigan, Lloyd had a ten-by-twenty Tuff Shed put up which he named "the barn."

I feel so blessed to have Lloyd in my life. He had spent his whole life living in Michigan and was willing to move to Arizona for my health. I was used to sand, cactus, and mountains from having lived in San Antonio and Colorado Springs. This move would be a totally new life for him since he had never lived in the southwest. No more blowing snow, deer hunting, and working on projects up there.

We drove home, put the fifth wheel up for sale, loaded his car hauler with a load of furniture, and came back to Tucson. We unloaded, reloaded with furniture from there, and headed back to the UP. Lloyd put the property up for sale and arranged to have an auction sale.

We were told property wasn't selling very fast and not to expect much for a while, especially when located on a gravel road and surrounded by woods. Three weeks after going on the market, we had a couple come to look at it. A short time later, we were notified that they would buy the property. The closing took place in August. They were the only people to look at the property. Divine intervention.

We had a huge auction sale on July 13. It should have been a two-day sale for all that we had to get rid of, but it was what it was. Lloyd had sold most of his big equipment privately before the sale, which was a blessing.

We loaded the rest of the furniture, his tools, etc., in a Penske truck, pulled a trailer with the Equinox on it, and headed for Tucson. We arrived at our new home on July 30, 2019, temperature on arrival was 106 degrees. Welcome to Tucson!

Our mobile home is sixteen by seventy, and our park is on an Indian Reservation. We love the area. We lived around boxes piled to the ceiling for about two and a half months as Lloyd tore out all the cupboards and replaced part of the kitchen floor. We ordered new cupboards, and it was nonstop work for Lloyd for a long time.

Jackie and Al had been attending Sahuarita First Church in Green Valley, and when things finally started to settle down for us, they invited us to their church. The first Sunday there, we knew that was going to be our church. No need to look any further. Pastor Dave and his wife, Joan, are awesome, and the people are all so friendly. We both felt so much at home. The church is Pentecostal. Al was Baptist; Jackie, Catholic; and I Lutheran. Lloyd and I exchanged our covenant commitment at a Mennonite church. How is that for variety? The main thing is we all worship the same God.

We were really getting acclimated to Tucson and with the GPS were finding our way around the city, mostly to doctor's appointments for Lloyd. We spent Thanksgiving at our home and had dinner in the clubhouse, which was really nice as we got to know more people. We spent Christmas Day with Jackie, Al, Tyler (Jackie's son), and Katrina (Tyler's wife).

We were still working on projects inside and outside of the house. Our new friends (snowbirds from Wisconsin) would play bingo, so we saw more and more of each other. While Lloyd worked on the house, Tom decided to paint Lloyd's barn. Still needing something to do, Tom then painted the outside of our house. How is that for a friend? We are looking forward to having Tom and Jane back here this fall.

Along came the coronavirus, and everything changed around the whole world for all of us. Since then it has been very quiet around the park, so other than going to church (with masks and following guidelines) and going to the store, it has been a very quiet life. Lloyd and I have spent a lot of time reading.

Looking back on my life, I realize how God has blessed me in so many ways. I have three healthy children, seven healthy grandchildren, and two healthy great-grandchildren. I have been blessed with a great and caring man like Lloyd and his three sons coming into my later life. Also Jackie and Al. Jackie has become my third daughter (I think of her as such), and Jackie calls me Mom (which I am honored to be).

We attend an awesome church. I have had big, beautiful homes in the past (as has Lloyd), but I have never enjoyed them as much and felt such contentment as I do in our sixteen-by-seventy mobile home filled with God and love.

My breathing is better (I can once again sing in church) and I walk a mile almost every morning. Eventually, I will be on oxygen. I am grateful for every breath I take. In the past six and a half years, Lloyd has seen fifteen doctors trying to find out what is causing all his back pain. The Lord has blessed us with a surgeon who has found the problem; Lloyd will be having corrective surgery in the next few weeks. Praise the Lord! We are looking forward to our trip back to Michigan to pick up his '52 Chevy two-door Bellaire hardtop (painted red), which should be ready for pickup soon.

Most of all, I am thankful for all the blessings our precious Lord has given us. We have been going through the coronavirus outbreak, observing all the rules, masks, and guidelines, as is the world. This too shall pass. Our country is in turmoil, but God is in control and *his* will be done. It is my constant prayer that the people and leaders in our country of America will turn back to God. Our founding fathers started this great country with God as their leader. If everyone would ask God for *his* help and guidance, we could once again have a great country. How blessed we have been.

Lloyd and I rely on God's guidance through books, the Bible, sermons, and friends. He hasn't let us down yet. We are looking forward to the day we will be in our best home yet. Our heavenly home. To God be the glory.

ABOUT THE AUTHOR

Shirley is a proud Christian who loves life. Like many, her life has been filled with sharp curves and potholes, mistakes and regrets, but through her challenges, she turned it all over to God. He is our Shield and Protector. Shirley's daily devotions are testimony of her promise she made to God.

She is extremely proud of her children and grandchildren and loves sharing treasured moments in their lives. She continues to inspire others and has brought God's word to many. Blessings continue to rain on her life in many ways. Shirley and her husband, Lloyd, currently live in Tucson, Arizona, which has provided much relief for her medical challenges.